AUTUMNAL HEART

The Collected Poems of Sue Scalf

Autumnal Heart: The Collected Poems of Sue Scalf
(soft-cover edition)
By Sue Scalf

© 2017 Sue Scalf

Published by PREMIUM PRESS AMERICA, Nashville, Tennessee

All rights reserved. No part of this book may be reproduced or transmitted in any form or by any means, electronic or mechanical, including photocopying, recording, or by any information storage and retrieval system, without prior written permission of the publisher, except where permitted by law.

ISBN 978-1-933725-42-0

Library of Congress Control Number: 2016952557

PREMIUM PRESS AMERICA books are available at special discounts for premiums, sales, promotions, fundraising, or educational use. For details, contact the publisher: P.O. Box 58995, Nashville, TN 37205, or phone toll-free 800-891-7323, or 615-353-7902, or fax 615-353-7905, or go to www.premiumpressamerica.com.

To arrange an interview with the author, contact the publisher.

Edited by Liz Reed

Text and cover design by Sara L. Chapman, Art Squad Graphics artsquadgraphics.com

Cover painting by Kathy Hartzog

Author photo by Liz Reed

Printed in the United States of America
10 9 8 7 6 5 4 3 2 1

DEDICATION

This book is dedicated to Allen Johnson Jr. and Liz Reed, with my deepest gratitude.

> *Poesy vinum daemonum*
> Poetry, the wine of devils...
> —attributed to St. Augustine

One of the fathers, in great severity, called poesy *vinum daemonum*, because it filleth the imagination, and yet it is but with the shadow of a lie...yet truth, which only doth judge itself, teacheth that the inquiry of truth, which is the love-making or wooing of it, the knowledge of truth, which is the presence of it, and the belief of truth, which is the enjoying of it, is the sovereign good of human nature.
—Sir Francis Bacon

FOREWORD

Once in a great while, a poet like William Blake or Emily Dickenson comes along and shows us—with a few magical words—how to connect with our own deepest feelings, with each other, with nature…even with God. Sue Scalf is such a poet. Her work affirms what it means to be human. It penetrates to the heart deeply and clearly, letting me know that I am not alone.

Reading a poem by Sue Scalf leaves me shaking my head and thinking, "Yes, that's the way it is!" Suddenly, in some magical way, I am connected.

—Allen Johnson Jr.

I was born, my dear, with an autumnal heart.
—Thomas Wolfe

AUTUMNAL HEART

Soft as mountains in the mist,
sharp as bittersweet and briar,
air touched with incense and spice,
autumn builds its annual pyre.
Upon every hill trees murmur tales.
Bronze and flame rise from hidden fires,
and stars seem closer to earth.
Let me warm myself in the coals
of yet another year, a golden swollen moon
and harvests of scarlet and grain.
Let me hear again the old seductions
of wind and rain, promises the winds tell…
whispering my name. Take my hand
and listen to the chatter of acorns,
the song of birch and oak,
the palaver of maple and the elegy
of wind-blown smoke. You will not hear
the first flake of snow, nor the prayer
the woods make as it falls.

CONTENTS

1 *I: Devils' Wine*
3 These Weeds
4 Autumn, Don't
5 Speak To Me
6 Aspects
8 Always Eve
9 Alabama Autumn
10 The Typing Pool
12 The Way I Write
12 Pay Telephone
13 Désolé
14 Dark Honey
15 Point, Counterpoint
16 Gone
17 The Key
18 Ignis Fatuus
19 Chalice
20 Mountain Child
22 My Thin Gold Grandmother
24 Mother to Child
25 For Lack of Words
26 Our Lives Are Tangled
27 Biology, Night School
28 Literary Tea
29 Massacre
30 To the Fittest in the Office
31 The Bond (For Leslie)
32 The Lesson
33 Splitting the Melon
34 Toadstools
35 Montage
36 Spindrift
37 The Tallow Tree
38 Death of a Tree
39 Show and Tell
40 The Memory Box
41 Ripples

42 Encounter
43 End of the Workshop
44 Bus
46 Death of a Critic
46 Ticket, $2.50
47 Storm
48 Before These Mountains
49 Autumn Aubade
50 Beginning
51 The River
52 End of August
52 A Simple Thing
53 Spring, Rain, Laughter
54 Aurora Borealis
55 The Pleiades
56 City Cemetery
58 The Waiting Room
59 Preserves
60 Wind Chimes
61 No Sanctuary
62 Absolution

63 *II: Ceremony of Names*
65 Blackstar
66 Live Coals
68 Returning
69 Early Autumn, 1944
70 Roadside Crosses
72 Funerals
73 Yellow Creek
74 Simple Things
76 Watercolor
77 Something's Out There
78 Leaven
79 Montgomery
80 The Radio

81	Remembering Zelda	119	*III: South by Candlelight*
82	The Baptist Ladies Travel to the Factory Outlets		
83	Yard Sale	121	Held in Amber
84	Hester and Arthur in the Twentieth Century	122	Perils of a Southern Gothic Childhood
85	It Isn't Poverty	124	Skate Song
86	Hawk Above the Highway	126	Nativity on Roosevelt Street
87	Susurrus	127	Night on Craig Mountain
88	Elemental	128	The Sorcerers
90	Hansel and Gretel at the Beach	129	The Last Drive-In in America Closes
91	Harvest	130	Fresh Laundry
92	Prodigals	131	Lost Trove: Appalachia
93	Days of the Crone	132	After a Long Absence
94	It Must Have Been in Autumn	133	Mountain Fog
96	Star Children	134	A Gift of Potatoes
97	Oxfordshire	136	A House Beyond Repair
98	Ceremony of Names	137	April Reunion
100	Strawberrie Banckes	138	Watermelon Moon
101	Household Accounts	140	The Source
102	Less Than Greek	141	A Scent of Green
103	Night Fishing	142	Alchemy
104	Haunted	143	Dangers Past
105	Time Capsule	144	Indian Summer
106	The Food Bearers	146	Carapace
107	Newspaper Photo, 1920	147	Libation
108	A Sea Journey	148	Fallow
109	November Rain	149	Magnolias
110	The Gentle Way of Earth	150	On Buying a Sprig of Quince
111	Absence	151	Only the Locusts
112	Furnished Tombs	152	Snake
113	First Father's Day	153	Mountain Battle
114	Night Cry	154	Spring Rain
115	Another Picture	155	Love and a Season
116	Ghost Story	156	Winterscape
117	Grace	158	Tao
118	Perspective, Powell Valley	159	Fool's Gold

160	To a Fertilizer Salesman from Laurel, Mississippi	198	What the Roses Say
161	The Baptist Ladies Meet at Quincy's	199	Voice Among the Trees
		200	What You Were
162	The Cheerleader	201	Vanishing
163	On Meeting a Chameleon in My Medicine Cabinet	202	At an Auction, Maybe
		203	A Whirling in the Stars
		204	Fishing for God
		206	On a Kentucky Hill
164	Instructions	207	Broken Trust
165	First Reader, Politically Incorrect	208	The Lost Children
166	Camellias	211	**IV: What the Moon Knows**
167	Conjunctions		
168	A Night of Bingo, Mountain City, Georgia	213	Hambidge Woods
		214	Whispers
169	Buffalo Bill at the Piggly Wiggly	216	Grass
		218	Adagio for Voice and Strings
170	February, '63		
171	Night College	219	To Love
172	Travelers	220	No Stolen Fire
173	Genesis	222	Patchwork
174	Good Water	224	Perception
175	Poetry Teacher	226	Orion
176	Facing the Audience	227	Intermission
178	Tongues of Flame	228	April 12, 1945
179	The Lovers	230	This Easter, Nashville
180	Cold Comfort	232	Ancient Fire: Kentucky's First House
182	Pagoda Village		
183	Circle of Light	234	Testament
184	Widows' Walk	235	Canticle in September
185	Feather in the Wind	238	Revisions
186	Night Watch	239	Beach Fires
187	Remembrance	240	Balm
188	Singing Where We Are	241	Christina's World
189	When Spring Touched with Fire	242	Cherokee Autumn
		243	Meditation at Summer's End
190	The Storyteller		
192	On Such a Day	244	Tidal Marsh
194	A Bouquet for Leslie	245	The Cedar
196	What the Wind Knew	246	Shepherds at Midnight Remember
197	An Empty Vase		

248	The Created	294	Love Out of Time, Out of Season
249	Ruffed Grouse Beneath the Picture Window	295	Signature: The Deep South
250	Frost Study	296	Feast
251	Wild Geese in Moonlight	298	For William Matthews
252	The Feather	299	Flash of Green
253	The Children of Summer	300	The Art of Winning
254	Another Room	302	Grace Notes
255	Tidal	303	Copper Harbor
256	Last Winter	304	First Song
257	Autumn Snow	305	When Birds Return
258	What the Moon Knows	306	Disappearances
261	Late Spring: The Widow Speaks	308	That October Night
262	Processional in Gray	309	Soundless
263	Silences	310	If I Were a Poet
264	Storm's End	311	Each Year and Always
265	Moss on the North Side	312	The History of a Yellow Leaf
266	A Turn of Seasons	313	Merlin on Poetry
		314	Beyond Survival
267	*V: Bearing the Print*	315	What Dreams May Come
269	All Those Mornings	316	A Winter Tea
270	Triptych for Autumn	318	White Marble
272	Winter Apples	319	Once More This Fire
274	Cool Water	320	Overnight the World Had Changed
276	Used Clothes		
277	The Traveler	321	*VI: To Stitch a Summer Sky*
278	Descendant		
280	Voices	323	What Stays With Us
281	Portent	324	In North Georgia Near Warwoman Dell
282	Bearing the Print	325	Each We Lose
284	August Morning	326	Standing Here I See Hills Beyond Hills
285	Test		
286	Old Sins	327	Karma, Kismet, Fate
287	Soliloquy of the Rose	327	Belief
288	Without Shelter	328	Hope
290	Winter's Tale	329	Field of Flowers
292	Revelation	330	The Witch of Winn-Dixie
293	Forgiveness		

331 To Stitch a Summer Sky
332 There Is a Land of
    the Living
334 Sunday Chicken, '42
336 The Blackened Hearth
337 Depths
338 A Twig Has Told Me
340 October Cortege:
    New Orleans
341 Vignette
342 Star Gazer
343 Hummingbird
344 Home
345 Stuff
346 Once More in Passing

347 *VII: Almost Home*
349 What Kind of Miracle
350 Flakes of Moonlight
352 Lord of All Seasons
353 Circumference
354 Aubade for the First Cool Day
355 Forgotten Song
356 Witness
357 I Am Cleaning Out My Life
358 Primal
359 The Fourth Witch
360 Nighthawks
361 Regret
362 Remember
363 Maybe the Way Death Is
364 Lilacs
365 Anniversary
366 Almost Home

367 *VIII: New Poems*
369 This One Day
370 Dichotomies
371 When the Ink Ran Dry

373 *Index of Poems*

I

Devils' Wine

Poesy vinum daemonum
Poetry, the wine of devils…
—attributed to St. Augustine

One of the fathers, in great severity, called poesy *vinum daemonum*, because it filleth the imagination, and yet it is but with the shadow of a lie…yet truth, which only doth judge itself, teacheth that the inquiry of truth, which is the love-making or wooing of it, the knowledge of truth, which is the presence of it, and the belief of truth, which is the enjoying of it, is the sovereign good of human nature.
—Sir Francis Bacon

THESE WEEDS

With open heart and open childlike joy,
I hurried and clutched them
drooping in my moist fist;
heart racing, with knobby knees flying,
I ran to her.
She took them and looked at me.
Why, they're weeds, she said,
and set them on the windowsill
above the sink.
Clover with crowded stems
and tops like red pine cones,
the goldenrod and dainty Queen Anne's lace—
weeds, I thought,
trying to decide whether to be hurt.
Then I saw the smile as she looked at them and me—
and I ran to gather more.

So all my gifts I bring
with open heart, in trust,
trusting you to understand,
and find you do.

Darling, here;
these are for you.

AUTUMN, DON'T

Autumn, don't be beautiful this year;
come not at all or come in rain and bleakness,
sodden branches, sodden sky.
Don't be beautiful.
Don't be autumn.
Once besotted with your splendor
I'll not imbibe again.
Your burning trees scorch me
for I am parched and brittle,
am dry and snapping at the stem.
I dread your long goodbyes....
You are like one who cannot take his leave
and make an end of it—
prolonging with lingering farewells
the inevitable.
Cruel, sweet, melancholy season—
you are too much; you're more than I can bear.
When you come you will not find me here,
for I shall remain untouched—
I shall burrow and hide,
'til the last leaf, the last butterfly.
One must endure, so I've been told...
I can't remember why.

SPEAK TO ME

We laugh and clown and never say
the reality behind the eyes;
we hide ourselves away in gaiety—
a better shroud has never been found—
a burial in banter.

We who know oh most of all
that time is the wind never caught;
we who know most of all
aridity and rain gone forever
should be more honest,
should be more articulate.

The world is silent enough;
there are enough locks, stones, tombs—
I'll give you the key…
open, please…hello, let me have your hat…
and if we have nothing to say,
let's say that.

ASPECTS

I.
Without guilt or guile
As naturally as children smile
With their souls open like their eyes,
As naturally as trees lean in the wind
Without an act of will
We leaned and touched in stillness,
And I who have so many words to say
Called you friend
And shattered the stillness.
There was no other sound but the rain—
A clean cold rain—
A gentle gift
Like the gift we gave
Each other.

II.
Weak with desire
I imagine my voice strung out along the wire
Taut like a plucked harp string
Vibrating in the air
And I am aware of cables, relays
And all the myriad intricacies that separate us—
An electronic tone
Echoing the distance,
Your voice grown more distant still,
And I who know your heart so well
Am mocked by this nihility
Where neither of us are—
Far better to speak to you from some other star
Or hear your voice in some nodding flower
And return your call, seeking you,
Our words weightless as the wonder we share.

Hear me in the stillness speaking:
Hello...
Are you there?

III.
Seeking in hate an opiate and finding none,
Bludgeoned to no oblivion in slow recall,
Blood blisters that do not shed—
The dying and never dead—
What device can blot out your touch—
What brace can bear the weight?
Not these bones brittle bent and small.
The threshold of pain
Is simply sweetness—in high intensity.
Memory becomes a child that sings itself
To restless sleep
Repeating stupidly,
Never again, never again, never again.

ALWAYS EVE

Space is everything outside the circle of this bed,
this room—
Eden is here   we two
the only man and woman ever created.
The universe exists out there somewhere in darkness
but I know none but this
the bright circumference of your arms
nor yesterday, nor tomorrow—
time condensed
and essence in a kiss
and life and death...

While candles flutter...   flame to incense
the moon thins to a Eucharist—
the night moves as a mist toward dawn.
The serpent waits outside the door.

ALABAMA AUTUMN

A Southern summer wears away as slowly as love dies
Or youth fades—
It is gone, we are old, and we did not feel the going,
Only the aftermath.
For no drama spangles the trees with scarlet and gold,
No drums beat nor snare drums roll—
But the cotton swells in the boll,
And the butterflies are here again.
The ache is in the air.
The locusts sing of loss in an off-key dirge
That tells of frost,
While flowers too tired to bloom
Leach and yellow from the roots.
Gourds droop and harden while the vine dies;
The grass has ceased to grow—
The sun has drawn the green away.
And today, I saw one leaf, then two,
    as if taken by surprise,
Detach themselves and attest their freedom to fly.
Cattails sway by turbid ponds where fat fish lie;
Burnt sienna creeps slowly in the heat.
Pine needles brown on the trees and whisper
In a wayward breeze that hints of arctic,
    bearing from somewhere
A subtle cold, an incense from the snow.
And there is intermission everywhere
As if the earth caught its breath
Looking back to see where it had been
And paused...
Held in a hush, a waiting, a pall—
A gradual exhaustion that calls itself
Fall.

THE TYPING POOL

She comes into the office with her granny dress,
Her long hair flowing loosely and we notice her—
She drops her head,
Though her dress proclaims she wants attention,
She really doesn't—
Then defiant, she tosses her hair and holds up her chin.
"I'm in."

Divorced, the mother of a three-year-old,
Craving attention, rebuffing it,
Do your thing.
Doesn't she look natural?
And tomorrow a mini mini or a maxi and platform shoes
Big as boxes, and all the rest.
And what she wants I know so well—
To be loved for herself, the golden kernel of herself,
Don't we all?—and to be ourselves, whatever that is,
And to toss our manes and lift our chins.
Do your thing.
Doesn't she look natural? Incense and macramé—
During the day a government job and a baby at home to
     be cared for,
But incense and macramé and wild wild beads
Ease the pain a little—
Ah don't I know,
And doesn't she look natural?
How wonderful it would be if this proclamation by dress
Were an outward sign of an inner freedom,
If we were, indeed, all free;
She isn't either, and I know it.
The telephone rings, the clock hand crawls,
The paint is flecking off the walls,
And we do our thing every morning,

Our duty to life's responsibility—
Some in old lady comforts, others in boots,
The shoes trudge up the stairs.
One woman is fat, another, bones;
And we plug ourselves in
With the Dictaphones.
Don't we all look natural?

THE WAY I WRITE

The way I write a poem is this:
Emotionally, without reason, reaching for beauty and depth,
Then slowly and sanely I pick it to death.

An analogy to love exists.

PAY TELEPHONE

I listened to that telephone ring
in an abyss of lonely time,
the call no one answers,
the story of my life
in echoing seconds a lifetime long,
picked my pride off the payment,
retrieved my dime,
and went on.

DÉSOLÉ

Lacking the substance,
lacking the depth, lacking the mercy,
not dark enough for death
but death's periphery
here in this twilight,
dirty, gray—
winter is beginning forever;
all the clocks stopped,
time fails and falls apart,
while sleet whispers in a thin drizzle.
No flood cleanses, no sun returns,
no tears fall, but something,
gnawing like a mouse on a dry heart,
fattens.
There is no sound but the sound of sleet
and tiny teeth.

DARK HONEY

I make dark honey
from grotesque blossoms
of deepest misery,
and suck the heart of summer
from froth and foam of flowering trees.
Blended through some subtle chemistry,
transformed through my own being
in weird alchemy, word by word
the globules of gold and amber form,
and contain both flower and me.
For winter's cold and barren need,
upon tumbled weeds and tortured dreams
I feed; and lightly, lightly sip on love until—
drunk on nectar, in studied ecstasy,
I make dark honey,
and survive,
as does the humble bee.

POINT, COUNTERPOINT

In the heart and heat of summer
    I feel the fall.
In all my happiest days I am aware
    of a darkness out of sight,
and in all love a touch of malevolence,
    in beauty—brevity, and in truth—
relativity....

Secure in my twenty-four-hour day,
    I remember this age may vanish
like the dinosaur, and I am aware
    of time beyond the clock,
that security is a word spun from
    spider webs melting in the sun...

yet
    what is heat without cold,
love without hate, and
    truth without a point of view?

Nothing stands alone—
    matter, anti-matter—
the poles hold each other up
    and the moon holds up the earth,
moontide-earthtide drawing each to each.

So what am I without you?

    I exist in your view and have my being.
Though without me the world dies,
    I live in your eyes.

GONE

The taste still upon my tongue,
I stare like a child amazed
at the empty cone,
watching sweetness melt away
on hard stone,
wondering that there is nothing to salvage,
wondering how loss can make me grow.
Tearless, benumbed, empty handed—
Having let love go,
I look up to see who's watching,
and manage a whistle as I walk away.

THE KEY

When I knew grief, living hurt,
beauty hurt,
and I swore nothing would hurt me anymore
that I could prevent, nothing but natural pain.
I could not prevent death or grief
but when they came
they would have to search me out—
for I would never seek love or beauty again;
no, I would lock the door,
and beauty would not hurt me anymore.
I heard the cold click of the key,
and I rested, weary and wary.
I knew the days would be long and dreary,
but I could live, I could stand to live.

And then one day, quite unaware,
I came upon an autumn tree
that took the very breath from me,
and out loud I exclaimed
and threw my arms about it as if it were a person;
spontaneously, freely, I held that tree
and looked up into its golden branches,
loving every glowing leaf, every sunlit bough,
taken in thrall by a beauty so bright it made me grow,
and stretch on tiptoe, reaching up, speechless now.
And slowly I knew then, I could never be different
than I had ever been;
ah I knew then, I would always greet life with open arms,
and whatever price, I must pay...
be love or beauty what they may.

IGNIS FATUUS

All my life I've sought iridescent things,
the fragile dream,
the shimmer of opaque wings of a dragonfly in the sun,
bare trees and each twig beaded with gleaming rain,
all the delicate things—
friendship so deep no words are needed, and unnecessary,
fox fire in deep woods when the moon rides high,
one autumn leaf with the sun shining through—
for me I knew these would do,
a distant star and rainbows where no rainbows are.

Blinded by the light shattered against a rushing stream,
deafened by the wind, and drone of bees,
in the midst of dreams I have not been unaware
of pain and ugliness, no, I have not been unaware
that while I stand and stare, behind my back a specter waits.
But these have made me keep my sight, my ears, my heart
full but never sated...
and I look elsewhere—
at pollen in the air.

Have you ever noticed a black pigeon's wings?
or his eyes?
Every feather is a galaxy...
And his eyes, buttons of flame....
Such burning, shimmering, lovely things
are found in the world of a fool
in a fool's paradise.

CHALICE

The early morning sky,
foggy and gray,
touches the sea
of green and slate,
heaving full and flat,
nearly silent;
earth, air, fire, and water
blend in a blue awakening.
The small waves whisper:

Still   still...
wait   wait....

A single gull
dances his way
around a crescent of foam
hissing into the sand;
the sea oats
bow their heads
and pray:

Still   still...
wait   wait....

Time gathers into pewter light,
brimming with quietness...
an absolute peace
too fragile to hold.

MOUNTAIN CHILD

The banjos and ballads are muted in the roar
And screams of road machinery, the blare and glare
Of hot dog stands, strip mines, and souvenirs,
And there is a brittle wisdom now, a subtle loss
Hard to define... as children debauched
Show innocence fled by a hard bright knowledge in the eyes.
So nothing now will ever be the same,
Yet
The mountains are there, aloof as ever, proud
And above reproach like a hardy people....
The mountains are there still, like memory,
Holding a knowledge, a secret of their own.

I remember cloud fingers over the hills,
Fog in the hollows,
Thin snows in winter—
And in spring, rain crows
And snows of laurel—
A persimmon moon in autumn,
Burning sumac and alder,
Bleak cabins and a winding road
    thick with dust—
Hazelnuts and chinquapins and black walnuts
And the sulphury green taste of water from
    the pump—dripping from a gourd,
Jar-flies at dusk in the trees,
    I remember these....
Paling fences, widow's tongue and wild asparagus
In coffee cans on porches,
The smell of salt pork frying, and
The aroma of mustard greens—
Damp rich earth, leaf mould and ferns near
Mountain springs—

Homely zinnias and drooping peonies in Grandma's garden,
Red-stemmed pokeweed, sorrel and clover by
  new plowed ground,
Cloud shadows passing over
Tall corn rustling in the wind—
All these I remember....
Moths beating against the screens,
The flicker of kerosene
And long shadows from the fireplace
Tracing patterns on the floor,
And tree shadows and screech owls
To people the foggy heavy-dewed nights;
Hants that roam graveyards and hollows,
And tall tales of panthers and strange lights—
All these I remember that have been
And will not come again—
Those I loved and little things,
Grandpa's brogans and shoestring ties,
His eyes, and the way he was always looking off
In distances, seeing something I could not see—
All these return to me...
And I who think I am rootless am aware
I am a part of this land from which I came,
This earth, these mountains, this dark and bloody ground
The Indian only visited.
I lived here, was born here—
These mountains hold my forebears' bones,
These mountains are my home.
I remember and for a little while...
I am a mountain child.

MY THIN GOLD GRANDMOTHER

They had to put a diaper on her. She was so thin you could see the separation of the bones in her arms. And when she died, she died alone in that rest home, sitting in her wheelchair.

Holding on until her body was gone,
unable to support the weight of the soul,
she lived until all her philosophies
were gone; and she had been through
the refiner's fire and nothing was left
of dross or impurity.
She lived to an age
past all reason to want to live,
until her brain was weighted
with the past, softened at the rim,
until her eyes were too dim to see
a bird, a tree, until her very body
was an insult to her; and all those she had given life
she did not recognize, until they
were a composite—one—
of all she had known and loved.
And they muttered to themselves:
"Why must she endure and drain us dry,
why can't she die?"
Although she couldn't hear,
it was in the air;
and she smiled sweetly and pretended
not to understand, or perhaps she did not
    understand.
She wore away—to thin thin gold;
she bore it all;
and when there was nothing left
except her innocence, her last breath
was still not a surrender, just a letting go.
And she let go of her own free will
and drew out the last of life

in a soft tired sigh called death.
And then she left....
Grandmother,
to your grandeur, to your spirit
I bow my head in awe and poverty—
remembering a fiery, molten filigree
like sunlight on the river.

Your death summed your life.

MOTHER TO CHILD

You hold the pink swirl
to the pink swirl of your ear
and hear the strange song
of a distant sea.
I share your wonder.
Though I know the reason,
it is no less a miracle.

Science avers
that in your ear—
those tiny bones beating,
anvil and stirrup—
live the remains
of an aquatic ancestor;
even the fetus,
swimming in a quiet sea,
forms gills.
Not in the conch, then,
but in the cochlea
the tide whispers,
ancient seas beat on ancient shores,
echo calls to echo.
So the song, my child,
is not in the shell.
It is in you.

Let me now in my cupped hand
hold this shell, and
we two, young and old, tattered remnants,
will share
this love reaching toward itself wave after wave,
this music,
this miracle.

FOR LACK OF WORDS

You asked me what I want
And I not knowing
And not knowing what to say
Laughed and said:
A loaf of bread,
A jug of wine, and thou.
And since I've had time to think
and knowing no more now
I think this answer must do—
Must say all I cannot say—
For I am so tired
Of a world of made and bought,
Tired of plastic and pretense,
And I want
To go back to warmer elements,
To the real, like the words
The lack of words between us.
You asked me what I want...
I want to love and feel and know
The weight of earth and sky,
To stretch my arms out,
To know my place in time—
I want everything:
A loaf of bread, a jug of wine,
And thou....
This is my answer—inadequate
And bare and saying less
Than words locked in my heart.
For lack of words—let me take your hand
And place it in mine.

Come sip the wine.

OUR LIVES ARE TANGLED

Our lives are tangled with turtles,
dogs, cats, kids, Hondas, and bills,
until we are inundated and suffocated,
caught up, submerged, laughing, talking,
swathed in smoke, the static of voices,
the crowds, the mad, the sad and lonely crowds,
until there is no room for you and me—
and yet across the room our eyes meet and speak
and everything falls away
to quiet repose, to a stillness that knows
the inmost core of the other;
an island in the center of an ocean's roar,
two eyes meet like hands that reach and touch
and we walk a deserted beach
alone once more.
Breathless, I clasp
a lifetime
shared
in one small stare.

BIOLOGY, NIGHT SCHOOL

The night he brought in a cat
Split from crotch to chin
I laughed and said: Prejudice.
The cat was black and female.
But oh the night he brought a human heart
I had to leave
I thought of Keats and Shelley;
I thought of you and me.

The right ventricle is enlarged
He said.
He probably had emphysema
And smoked too much.

What did he look like
Chain smoking those cigarettes;
What did he feel?
Now his heart on display
To students making stupid remarks.
Failing the study of life,
Do I fail life? Well, then I must.

My heart too tender, on display
In its way—
Out there for all to see—
Jokes choked in my throat
I had to leave.

LITERARY TEA

The muscles tight, the jaws taut,
A natural consequence of unbearable tension
Hidden very well.
A matinee performance.
The mouth spoke and said the appropriate words,
The eyes with the proper expression
Made their comments of interest and attention.
        Yes, is that so?
        Two lumps, no cream.
        Well, in my opinion...
And the mind, oh, anywhere but there,
The words piling up like thunderheads
Whirling in the brain, pressing to get out,
Words hardly expressible,
Half-formed in the midst of that crowd—
While one pair of eyes meeting mine deeply
Aroused a tingling recognition, quickly veiled.
        Well, his poetry is far superior...
        No more for me, thanks.
        That *is* delicious.
What a farce we live. How we hide ourselves
In polished acts of insincerity, building fences
To shut the world out, ourselves in,
For the sake of bloody appearances.
Trembling hands betraying
Speak a volume in Sanskrit no one can translate.
And the teacups clatter like laughter with an edge.

MASSACRE

It was such a casual conversation;
I took my pride and made a fortress of words,
And laughter hid wounds like moats;
I never lowered the drawbridge of myself.
And this is what I wanted to do:
Never having been able to make you suffer,
Not once,
I wanted to hide my suffering and did—
Only I knew and know
The catapult, the Trojan horse,
    the battering ram,
The small revenge of a bored yawn.
Safe in a bastion of self-sufficiency,
I wrested the triumph from you,
Yet only I
Felt the death blow.
It was a small massacre
As massacres go.

TO THE FITTEST IN THE OFFICE

Not afraid of nature, just human nature,
I fear less the serpent in the grass
than the one behind the desk;
and I fear less the claws and fangs nature knows,
camouflage to protect and hide
for the sake of life,
not hurt for the sake of hurt,
not blood for sadism's sake.
The heart that nature breaks
is broken surely, yet the weapons
hurt less in the motive
of the need to survive.
One must keep alive in either world
where the snakes are disguised.

THE BOND (FOR LESLIE)

Overly protective you say?
I do not protest.

Instantly alert,
I hear them far away—
the shrill, hard wail
of sirens.

> My child is on a bike!
> My child is in a car!
> And if not mine, someone's,
> someone's child is in pain.

The screams stop—then move on.
I join the silent bond
of all mothers
who pray.

Child, you cannot know love's burden…
yet.

THE LESSON

I sat upon his lap, happy
in his love until
she took me aside and explained
the ways of dirty old men,
even uncles.
After that I always measured motives;
I was aware.
Such a small destruction.
One must warn young daughters.

Now
my voluptuous blue-jeaned daughter
sits upon her uncle's lap,
arms entwined about his neck.
Dark whisperings rustle in my brain
quietly as a snake in dry leaves
gliding from a lost Eden.
The wind sweeps through the curtains,
cleanly.

> He has children her age.
> We only see them once a year.
> I will not.
> I will not.

Mother,
dead these many years,
I forgive you.

SPLITTING THE MELON

The melon stealers know
that knives sever,
but there is a quicker way
to reach the center
where beaded sweetness waits
in cloisters of coolness.

There is a quicker way
to pierce the skin,
to savor musky earth,
the pale green rim,
to drink the red water
dear to marauders.

Knives sever,
but knives are tame and slow.
The melon eaters know.
They hurl the melons down.
The heart splits
with one swift blow,
a sound of sucking air.

TOADSTOOLS

In woods and fields
Spilling its incense
A dusty gray—
Have you ever touched
A certain round ball
And watched it turn to smoke?
It propagates that way.
The devil's powderpuff
I've heard it called,
Just a toadstool
Shattered with a stroke.
So what once seemed real,
Such an everything to me,
A mystery,
An all touched with maybe,
Now it has been,
Puffs to nothing.
Dreams are made never to be
Lost in achieving;
Realized, being less
Than a mist and gone.
Never touch
The devil's powderpuff,
To dream is enough,
More than enough.
Only fools
Kick dreams to toadstools.
Walk on.

MONTAGE

Standing at the door
looking back for the last time,
I knew it was the last time;
we stared in that second that held
for an eternity,
and I saw not just one
in that hospital bed
but a whirl of images superimposed.

I could hardly remember
Great Grandmother—when she died,
but I did remember falling leaves,
September,
and seeing her on that bed
in that little house.

The image came back,
and another image, another look;
generations of faces stared up at me,
a circumference, an arc, a wheel,
and strangely I saw my own face there....

I held the door and said inadequately:
"Goodbye" and turned away.
For I had seen—leaden-tongued, what can I say?—
bravery, strength, transcendence,
an illusion of time, a heritage of steel,
the commonalty of all things
and the beauty of all...
all light all love all mystery
in burning eyes across the years...
and more than this.

I know there were no tears.

SPINDRIFT

High in the tall old trees,
the pecan, the elm,
the October wind soughs
like the sea.

I stand with my feet in dead leaves
listening
and hear
the heaving pulse of tides.

A curled leaf loops downward
without a sound or sigh,
while far above the wind moans
and swells, pouring by.

Leaf spray, salt spray,
the sting and ache
are all the same,
the source is all the same…

autumn breaks in waves
whispering goodbye.

THE TALLOW TREE

for H., dying of cancer

The tallow tree is leafless now,
leaves spread under it like pools of wax.
Covered with seed pods, the popcorn flowers,
in the irony of a November thundershower
it stands like an affirmation—
as if it were spring, as if it were blossoming—
a white flame, a white tongue of flame
warming the rain.
I stand at my window and stare.
Something in me wants to translate;
the words elude me, skitter away, come back again....
White tree, mist of frailty and strength,
defying all outward evidence of seasons,
in the midst of death making the grand gesture,
though my naked limbs send forth no bloom
in tender paradox,
tallow tree beckoning in November rain,
I know you.
We are kin.

DEATH OF A TREE

That sound
Like a pickaxe on hard ground
Like someone digging a grave—
The echo of coldness.
Every thud seems to arouse some fear,
Distant rolling thunder,
A green-black sky,
Dread without a name…
The blunt steel blade
Reverberating into hollowness,
The numbed hurt beyond a scream,
The falling edge of a dream,
And an end…
The final rip and tear,
A rush of air,
A thump,
A brittle break of limbs
    like little sighs—
A whimper of leaves
And then nothing.
The blankness hurts the ears
Repeating: nothing, nothing.
The stillness grieves.
No bird sings.

SHOW AND TELL

Someone related to me
How a child told the class,
"Mommy and Daddy had a party
And this morning I stepped
Over bodies to come to school."
I laughed—
And then I thought of the child I was,
Now fled—
How every morning I step
Over the bodies half-dead
Of yesterdays, how we all pick our way
Over all the mistakes,
Dead weight like empty bottles,
How no school can explain
The gray knowledge of years and fears,
The erosion of innocence,
The cynicism that sprouts like briars
Where once flowers grew,
Three-martini love affairs,
Dust in the mouth, dust in the soul—
Parched tears, all the sad debris
We know and show, oh show so well …
But never never tell.

THE MEMORY BOX

Scraps of paper, pictures,
Dried flowers—
I cannot revel in past
Happiness   youth   hours
Old hurts, old animosities,
Musty griefs that yawn to life,
The lived-through days I've shed
In slow metamorphosis of years.
It's as if I were burying myself alive
In the rubbish of old diggings;
Old bones in bat-filled caves,
Forgotten names in autograph books
Saying "Remember me,"
Powder, crumbling in my hand.
Leave it alone; don't stir the dust.
Put the memory box back in the attic,
A feast for silverfish and mice,
For other small creatures
That need to survive....
It's over and
Thank God.
If the dead arise
One judgment will suffice.

RIPPLES

Like children,
we stood by the river skipping stones.
I felt as ponderous as Goliath,
as inadequate as David.
You talked of people
using people,
using general terms,
your words slick as pebbles.
I said, "People are like that,"
but you tried to deny such things
    exist,
the guilt you were feeling
    making you defensive.
I smiled my crooked smile,
the one I put on when someone
    tries to put me on,
the smile that's directed inside
    to a joke I tell myself.
For even then I knew—
I had my eyes open always,
feeling the heft and weight, hearing
the flat splat of sinking stones.
Now with the incredible smoothness
    of not caring,
I fling this poem at you....
Skipping on edge it sings
    and vanishes.

ENCOUNTER

Suddenly, looking in the mirror,
the eyes stare back startled;
the toothbrush stops in mid-air.
Something is beating like wet wings
starting to stir.
Something wants out.
Trapped inside this stranger's flesh,
I am aware.
Within this pretense of blood and bone,
something is separate. It is what I am.
It moves; it whirrs.
Suddenly afraid, I watch the hand tremble,
putting the toothbrush in the rack. Detached,
the hand grabs a glass. The sane, antiseptic taste
of morning mouthwash draws me back
into numbness. Yet something lingers.
I avoid the mirror, the face.
The silence hums like the ghost of wings.

END OF THE WORKSHOP

While she argued the inviolability of the sonnet,
ozone thinned and earthquakes rumbled;
galaxies collided over our heads;
vast armies gathered,
rank on rank,
with drawn swords.
While she argued the inviolability of the sonnet,
the sun darkened and the moon turned to blood;
civilizations fled from the rooftops and the fields;
graves opened,
and the sea spewed forth its dead.
When she looked up blankly,
her voice echoed in an empty room—
"I refuse to accept such a definition.
The sonnet remains the same," she said.

BUS

Here is life packed tightly,
Hurtling down a slash of asphalt,
Slicing through clay banks of new highways,
Life smelling of diesel, sweet-sour flesh,
Cigarettes, cokes and gum,
Sleeping, talking, twiddling its thumbs,
Looking at the scenery with a numbed interest.

>Stranger,
>I will tell you my life story
>between Cleveland and Cincinnati.
>
>I am sure I love you though we've
>just met.
>
>I wish that nut would turn down that
>transistor.
>
>I'm going to Tupelo to see my sister.
>Her husband's got the dropsy.
>
>Look at those long-haired guys.
>Look like girls.
>
>Those Afros... I expect to see
>little birds flying out.

And the stations smelling of soap and disinfectant,
Food and sweat.
A two-A.M. waitress snaps out:
"I've only got two hands,"
And slaps down a plate of resentment,
While the pinball machine rings and mingles
With the dispatcher's voice...

>Cincinnati, Covington, Lexington,
>Knoxville, with connections for...

Ding ding whirl

The flying saucer machine lights up
And takes off, standing still.

    Say, have you got any change?
    Don't worry you can use it after me.

    Ha—they charge you. You should
    charge them for using these johns. And
    never any soap.

    You hear about the woman had a baby
    in this bus station?

    God... imagine.

Outside, the air seems cold
And fresh, though touched with
Fumes and sadness.
It is quieter.

    Goodbye, take care, have a nice trip,
    see you next year.

    Say, hon, don't sit next to him.
    He smells like beer.

    I love you, take care, goodbye.

The driver tears the ticket off,
Without expression.
And the bus rumbles and vibrates.
We straighten our skirts, loosen our ties,
Let the seats back, light-up and sigh.

Leave the driving to us—
Leave the world rushing by—
Caught between here and there.

We're all on a bus
Bound for somewhere.
We're all on a bus...
Bound for somewhere.

DEATH OF A CRITIC

I met death,
Smelled his fetid breath,
Touched his tainted hand.
You're awfully trite, I said,
Why you're nothing but a cliché—
The oldest story I ever read,
Told and retold.
I thought you, at least,
Would be something new.
Death looked back at me and laughed,
Reaching for my throat, shutting my mouth.
But not before I managed to gasp:
After all,
The whole thing's been done before.
But death just laughed.

TICKET, $2.50

We come spilling out into the light, blinking;
We avoid each other's eyes, feeling a little naked.
My stranger's face, reflected in a mirror,
Stares back at me without recognition.
Longing for Tara, I walk out into the city streets, alone,
Slip the key in the ignition,
And drive the wagon through burned fields of corn.

I'll never be hungry again.

There are other sorrows than war, than lost loves.
Ah Scarlett, there are no Rhetts in this world.

STORM

The cinnamon cat is curled
in a snug ball of sleep.
    Safe in a warm house
      one is unaware of black night stalking;
      one is unaware of cold rain.
I have taken the jungle from the cat:
de-clawed, de-sexed,
he is afraid of the outdoors.
I love him.
I had an outside cat, black as despair;
he let me feed him twice a day
and pat his bony frame
until he disappeared.
I respected his cool disdain.
    Safe in a warm house
      one is unaware of black night stalking;
      one is unaware of cold rain.
The cat at the hearth
rouses sleepily
hearing the storm;
something gleams in his eyes.
The fire reflects in both our eyes;
the fire claws and spits.
We lift our heads and stare at each other,
the cat and I. His tail flicks.
The walls contract;
rain hisses down the chimney
and scratches at the door.
    Unease breathes from the rafters.
Outside,
    lightning splits a universe
    dark as the heart of a panther.

BEFORE THESE MOUNTAINS

Landlocked, I find sharks' teeth in sand....
Here where the mountains run, an ocean ran
ten millennia before this life began.
Overhead the sky stretches
its thin illusion of blue
and here I hold shards of those who swam
an eon or two before these mountains
now cresting wave on wave, shadowed
in dim valleys and purple ravines.
In my hand, time narrows to bone.
My heart is a bone picked clean
by earth and sand,
and all my tears
are scattered in the wind.

AUTUMN AUBADE

Mist of midnight, warmed by the sun,
burns its frail heart upon the lawn,
lifts, and is gone to the river.
Rising there, it touches the trees
where yellow leaves drowse away
the mellow end of summer
in quiet sighs of slumber.
As if the world were sleeping cold
and restlessly stirs awake—
reaching for blankets of gold,
day breaks.

BEGINNING

Before you could really talk
You had learned—who taught you?—
To shrug your shoulders, open
    your hands and say:
"All gone."
And in those shoulders, that gesture,
    that spreading of hands—
There was such a loss—such an opening—
As if "All gone" were an opening.
I wonder why? Somehow it teases me,
    it tears me
That you could know so much, so early.
I think of your Great Grandfather
    when he died,
How he said, "It's over," and opened his hands.
I wonder if this loss, this opening,
Is a gesture we are born knowing,
A language we are born knowing…
Surrender or resignation… the beginning of
    the philosophic mind?
I only know, in the presence of those plaintive
    hands, those innocent eyes,
I cannot talk.
I cannot understand
The complete definition of loss,
The abyss between those hands.

THE RIVER

Daughter of rain,
Bearer of commerce,
Weaver of dreams,
Sliding in silence
You shatter the moon, ribbon the sun,
And sing the secret.
Earth's veins, earth's blood,
Sculptor of canyons, builder of deltas,
Hidden in mist, washed in light,
Swollen in flood—
You chant the secret.
Lover and destroyer,
Primeval mother,
Gentle healer,
Winding like a lost dream
Forever—
You whisper the secret
We almost know—
The deepest rhythm…
Earth's heart beating…
The flow that blends to width and breadth,
To salt of tears and seas.

END OF AUGUST

These are the termite days
insidious as decay,
the dry rot, the musty yeast,
the sweet powder of old women's cheeks,
the stale air of empty closets, closed rooms,
stairs leading to nowhere, no one at home,
the long, slow, endless hours
that gnaw to yellow dusk,
white wings in white dust....
These are the termite days,
hushed as death feeding.

A SIMPLE THING

As it began—
my hand slipped into yours
and it was hello—
so it ends,
if it can ever end:
my hand slips into yours again—
two lives touching like two hands
    warm palms pressed,
    flesh meeting flesh...
two lives touching,
holding,
then letting go.

SPRING, RAIN, LAUGHTER

You make me feel
light as spring—
you know what I mean—
spring with its sticky buds
and the feathery green,
spring with its wanton giving,
and open arms.
You make me feel
clean as rain—
you know what I mean—
tiny droplets hanging from leaf and bough,
rain cupped in a flower.
I think it's because of laughter,
the ringing soaring laughter
that makes us one,
light as spring, clean as rain,
fluid, frail, and silvered in the sun.
You know what I mean.
I know you know.

> *Stellar death throes fill space with stardust from which new stars and planets are born. It may come as a shock to learn that nearly all the atoms in your body were once part of a star that exploded and disintegrated, and that probably those same atoms were once the debris of still an earlier star.*
> —Kenneth F. Weaver, "The Incredible Universe,"
> National Geographic, May, 1974

AURORA BOREALIS

Out there, in that cold sky,
cold curtains sway and speak.

Life. Splitting from every amoeba,
tongued by every leaf and tree,
the heartbeat pulses from every pulsar in space.
Propelled from the womb
into this circumstance we never sought,
life uncurls in fingers and toes,
the budding, the breeding;
the heat of compost and decay
sends up a flame;
a great arc spirals from the sun;
electrons and protons collide,
drape the purple void in ice,
in burning ice.
Hushed.
Hanging.

And all matter is no less,
is but another name.

We are no less.

We are the dust of stars.

THE PLEIADES

It was a honeyed spring, dripping gold.
Five miles into the mountains we rode our bikes,
Nymphs and sylphs with bandaged knees and
    skinned elbows.
Lungs aching, thighs trembling, we threw ourselves upon
A grassy knoll, and screamed our delight
Breathlessly to a sky where no stars bloomed or burgeoned.
Our bodies were green and new as young grass,
Lithe as the woodbine;
Our blood sang in our ears.
The words we shouted, the laughter,
Are now sound under water, distorted and strange;
Only the essence remains,
That, and the apple trees across the road.

Alone, I walked into their midst,
Into trees burdened with bloom and alive with bees,
As if the trees themselves were humming.
"They're the Seven Sisters," someone called.
Sunlight filtered on freckled arms;
Sunlight and color swam and drifted downward
Into a petaled whirl of sound and scent.
I looked upward into the boughs,
Then turned backward to the knoll and hills.
Time clicked into a photograph.
Indelible. Still.

Now, when I see the Pleiades
I think of apple trees rooted in the earth
Like stars rooted in the sky,
And remember a spring—apple-green and warm—
And delicate apple-girls forever young,
Frozen in sunlight on a green hill.

CITY CEMETERY

Here,
dark-veined leaves fall
on pruned Bermuda grass and gray cement.
Death is impersonal and far away.
But I know a wild and ragged hill
where weeds contend with last year's leaves.
Dark-veined leaves fall among the brambles
and sunken stones
where a black snake suns.
Oak limbs open toward the sky
like some praying patriarch;
and one forgotten pioneer,
buried there,
has a pine tree rooted in his heart.
There, the wind spins hieroglyphs
in whisperings of parchment-thin old voices,
faint scratchings of lost words, lost worlds.
Strange, how wind and weeds offer comfort,
strange comfort in the simple cycle of
falling leaves and sun-warmed stone.

Here, where blood-red leaves fall
on pruned Bermuda,
no hearts live in living wood.
Love is locked away
beneath clipped grass, beneath cold steel.
Yet, at my feet a chickweed splits concrete.
A chickweed!
And in the Mayan jungle
vines engulf a temple.
How small the force
that rolls aside the doors of tombs,
how small the laugh
that strips an emperor.

Even in this lifeless plot
something seeks the light,
something will not be still,
a little laugh of truth sprouting
like comfort found in weeds
and wind and leaves,
and peace in the slow turn
of centuries and seasons.

THE WAITING ROOM

There you sit, gentle anachronism in a chrome and
    vinyl chair.
Eight floor tiles between us span a chasm.
Hating to stare, I fidget, look around the room,
but I am drawn to you,
drawn to your purple sun-bonnet.
Do you know we have been to the moon?
Crossed ankles encased in thick stockings
swollen above old lady comforts,
arthritic hands rest palms upward.
They are carved wooden flowers.
Your hooded eyes are calm.
And upon your head that burning bonnet,
    that glowing bonnet,
a pivot of color in a colorless room.
Archetype, earth mother,
my intellect strings words my heart ignores.
In this air-conditioned tomb
you are a summary of summers past,
redolent of hollyhocks and zinnias,
sweet mint and sassafras.
I snub out my Virginia Slim
and observe my nervous hands.
They are naked, plastic flowers.
And I am tired.
I ache to lay my head upon your ample breast.
How can I live in this world
when there are no purple bonnets left?
The nurse calls my name and a number,
assigning me my cubicle.

PRESERVES

She offered cucumbers and a recipe,
in loving endless detail, explained
the mysteries of canning.
I took her gifts with embarrassment.
How could I tell her?
How explain my vats are brined with poems?
I have my jewels in jars. Relish. Mincemeat.

Time is drying the vine;
windfalls waste in my cellar.
Preserving is heavy work.
I sweat. I hurry.
There is so much to hoard against the winter;
there are hungers to feed.

Holding to the light
this sweet-sour harvest,
my mouth puckers.

The frost is gathering,
and the grasshopper sings.

I must be at work, pickling.

Pickling.

Pickling.

WIND CHIMES

A crystal carapace descends—
a thin shield of words and laughter
words will not penetrate.
Meanings skitter on the edge,
slide away and disappear.
And yet I know, I feel,
the surface will give way—
to breeze and rain,
to a wordless tracery
of leaf-light and fern-shade,
to all the silent ways of speech.
And then, my friend, I'll touch you,
touch you with trembling fingertips.
And the wonder of it
will be like light,
will be like laughter
rippling
in tiny tinklings
of joy—delicate wind-chimes
touching   touching
in the faintest fragility
of song.

NO SANCTUARY

Autumn is here again.
I shall go mad!
I shall howl at the swollen moon—
Snatch at the leaves to save them—
Every one.
I shall drape thistles in my hair,
Fill my arms with milkweed, pampas, and tares.
I shall run crying down the streets.
Autumn is here again.
Autumn is here.
Autumn is here.

ABSOLUTION

Legs apart, feet firmly in the sand,
I stand and face the sea,
and I open like a window
the wind blows through.
Far away, a dipping gull genuflects
in fading light.
The waves swell and throb a Gregorian chant,
recede as small shells click like beads,
and I open like a window
the wind blows through.
A star or two flickers faintly as votive candles
or the heart of a sanctuary light;
sea spray tastes of tears,
but lighter, cleaner.
Mea culpa, mea culpa,
dark, heavy words have no place here.
Father, it has taken so many years,
but I have learned to love myself a little.
A thin moon appears.
And I am a window the wind blows through.

II

Ceremony of Names

BLACK STAR

The sun was a carbide lamp
leaving the valleys in shadow,
touching the tipple and the trees
with a sham of light.
Smoke from the chimneys of shotgun houses
clung close to the ground.
Frost flowered on the panes of the company store
where chalk dogs and garish lamps
blossomed inside.
In the shafts the rich seams
gleamed coldly as starlight.
The mines smelled of decay:
the detritus of dinosaurs and rotted leaves.
Tomorrow the coal would be trucked outside
to horizons beyond these hills.
There were no horizons here.

I left on the L&N,
listening to the wheels singing and clacking,
the derisive hoot of the whistle
curling like dark smoke backward,
past the Friendly Cafe, the Universal Garage,
the neon sign blinking EATS.
Horizons rolled ahead,
seas bluer than these mountains.

It has been years since then,
yet I return, pick in hand,
to mine the bitumin of memory,
to dig for what I was,
for something permanent as fossils, as ferns
pressed into anthracite,
the dark seams of time.

LIVE COALS

> *A place that ever was lived in*
> *is like a fire that never goes out.*
> —Eudora Welty

I.
She made a ritual of it,
fetching at bedtime the apples
from a sack in the pantry.
Mottled and flecked, the color of rubies,
in her hands
they seemed more than apples.

Cutting them with his pocketknife
as we sat before the fire,
he handed me the wedges one by one,
crisp and cold and good,
while outside was winter,
Appalachian snow as thin as shoe soles.
But I was a child who did not know
we were poor or that there was a world
beyond shuck ticks and apples at bedtime.

He told stories of bear hunts and wolves,
sang of coming around the mountain.
Grandma quoted nonsense rhymes.
I watched the fire,
unaware that time howled at the corners
and clawed at the door, unaware
that time would enter even here.
The coal in the grate shifted, flared;
the room glowed with the red light of apples.

II.
I cup a wavering flame
and breathe it to life
as he did on those mornings,
holding a newspaper over the grate,
making it draw until the tug of the updraft
pulled paper scorching to a blaze,
while in the kitchen she shifted the damper,
poked coals, clanged lids,
until the cast iron stove warmed again.
All the fragrances of winter and home
blended in heat and cold.

The yellow flame of the sun
spilled over the mountain
and through lace curtains,
sliding frost from the windows
in watery gold.
Roosters crowed, shadows
scuttled across the frozen pond,
and ducks ran flat-footed toward the grain.
Over the coldest years,
the warmth of voices calls me again
through the smoky edge of sleep.
Secure, I awake at home,
though it is gone,
and all I loved now lie in darkness.
Day begins.
The fire crackles and roars.

RETURNING

The moon spills its silver over the hills.
The moon is the same,
though flux and change leave little alone.
Still I return to sunlit summer days,
green summer days and home....

Follow me where a mountain stream
sings down a gorge, mists the stones with moss.
Wade water so cold your feet ache.
See a snake doctor hover like a helicopter,
leaving the tip of a weed quivering.
Break honeysuckle and drink
the clear nectar from the stem.
Then take my hand and listen...
from somewhere far away
the watery gurgle of a rain crow,
lonesome as a cabin empty these many years.
Hear the jar fly's dirge,
wailing "Summer, summer."
Taste the drops from the weeping willow
and stand above the marble markers;
read the names, the dates, in dying light;
hold memory gently;
then let it go,
       winging
               toward the moon.
The moon is closer than home.

EARLY AUTUMN, 1944

Afternoon heat and boredom send me
to the back porch to watch
Grandma wring a chicken's neck
for the Sunday crowd.
The chicken is dead with the first pop,
but its body is slower,
reflexing in spasms all over the yard.
It's the only death I have ever seen.

Inside the house
the Gothic radio is playing,
the voices from here a staticky hum.
Gabriel Heatter or Kaltenborn with doomsday tones
recites the evening news—a burst of laughter—
Gildersleeve perhaps.
With nothing to do, I swat flies
on the porch, planning their funeral,
then pile them in little heaps
like raisins.
A newsreel scene.
In the kitchen the icebox smells of sour milk,
and a dagger of ice melts in my hand
and drips on the linoleum.

I wander to the front porch;
the screen door squeaks asthmatically
and slams;
the swing sings in rhythm
to the high, sad swell of jar flies,
locusts. The sky is blood.

ROADSIDE CROSSES

For Harrison Mays, 1898–1985,
who placed the crosses

On banners across the mountain gorges,
on stones along clay banks,
then on crosses around a hairpin curve,
smiting like a guilty conscience,
cutting off laughter,
dire warnings loomed in rain and fog
or amid wild flowers and clover:
JESUS CHRIST IS COMING SOON,
GET RIGHT WITH GOD.

Through the grimy windows of the L&N,
above the click of the wheels,
above the coal trucks' grinding gears,
the shouts of undershirted men,
the laughter of girls joy-riding on running boards,
concrete crosses thundered their message,
a splinter in the brain,
a hangnail of the spirit,
more real than union wars
or tent revivals,
tangled snakes in coal oil light.

For fifty years,
hushed as pellegra,
silent as rickets,
quiet as God, he worked,
erecting the crosses
from Tennessee to Texas,
while, up mud-rutted hollers,
children's bellies swelled
and moonshine beaded in fruit jars.

When all obsessions ended,
a few crosses remained,
one in rusty chains
in his yard,
and a thousand lined the roads.
Tangled in kudzu and next to Burger Kings,
they weather, but the words
chill the summer air:

              P
              R
   TO MEET GOD
              P
              A
              R
              E

FUNERALS

We played at it then,
buried the cats and dogs
and assorted pets
with pomp and childish circumstance,
but we were untouched by death,
only curious.
The summers were sticky with heat and growing;
the days, long.
At twilight we told ghost stories,
ran home with pounding hearts
to catch fireflies and put them in fruit jars.
Days later we buried even these,
swathed in cotton in matchboxes.
I sang; Jerry delivered the eulogy.

Now into middle age we hardly know each other's names.
We've swathed our dreams in the cotton of contentment.
The petit mals, the little deaths of time,
have played their games with all our lives,
and we have known real ghosts,
scarier than those of forty years ago.
Though a ceremony seems in order,
who has a voice to sing
for a childhood that is gone?
And who, my little friends,
can carve the stone?

YELLOW CREEK

The years bead away like drops
and I am there once again
in collarbone-high creek water.
Unable to swim,
I cling to a dead willow
in muddy water ablaze with June light.
I am naked as Eve
before she sinned,
one of four girls in water
    warm as a bath
      delicious as honey
      silky on the skin
the dazzle of light in the swift flow
going by like time
going by like being sixteen:
wonderfully wet, alive and
unaware of the drought to come,
of the garden barred.
Here in September it is dry
but down the dusty years,
I hear the splash and screams,
hear the laughter light as air.
I see a swirl of green,
the preening of a dragonfly,
water skaters in spidery glides,
and from the distance of time,
light, keen and cold,
in the copperhead's eye.

SIMPLE THINGS

It was our ritual,
coffee and pound cake on the porch
in the late afternoon.
Thin and frail, you held the cup
in trembling hands,
saying, "Coffee never tastes so good
as when I have it here with you."
The days leading here needed no retelling.
We reveled instead in the peaceful porch,
the taste of coffee and cream.

Potted plants covered the rails with ferns,
widow's tongue and wild asparagus;
morning glories grew on strings.
Inside, beyond the dark screens,
the house held the heat,
smelled of camphor and mildew,
Estee Lauder and sickroom.
Linoleum buckled, plaster cracked,
and the closets were dark pits.

But in the yard cannas and peonies spread,
and sprawling maples offered shade.
The click of our spoons, the rattling cups
were lost in the locusts' rising whines,
the insect sounds of a dying summer.
Heads bent, we sipped, broke cake,
spoke softly or not at all.

I have a porch now, Grandmother,
not unlike yours,
where jasmine and trumpet vines
attract hummingbirds.
You would have liked it.
Sometimes I have coffee there,
and I never feel alone.

I hold you warm
like the cup in my hand.

WATERCOLOR

Sunset reflects off the eastern sky,
backdropped with dark clouds,
a line of trees bending before a thunderstorm.
White egrets in formation, flakes of silver,
hurry before the clouds: slate-gray and rolling
above cotton fields that glow
brighter, greener, at the storm's approach.
Walls of rain cracked by lightning behind
a dust-blowing wind
cleanse the world of color.
Twilight settles in
as the world becomes the
    center
of a gray, wet pearl.

SOMETHING'S OUT THERE

for Ceci

Promptly as if on cue the cicadas begin.
We close the door, build our fire,
trying to shut out what is out there,
with music and wine, guarded laughter.
Earlier we stood in the clearing
listening to something foraging,
the whispery rustlings like little breathings,
a snapping twig. They might be going in,
tired as we, or emerging on nocturnal prowls.
They are invisible, used to fear.

Yesterday, rangers warned of boars,
and today you found a bear track near the reservoir,
found spoor. The boar's skull on the mantle
was here when we came, but we perched the apple
between his tusks. He looks as if he wants to laugh,
but the candlelight flashing in his empty sockets
is demonic. We read, talk till time for sleep.

All night I hear a faint patter of rain on leaves;
it isn't raining. Something is moving.
One night you said you heard one animal
kill another. I remember that now,
imagine its frantic scream.
Once I cry out animal-like in my sleep,
caught in the jaws of an evil dream.

The moon through the branches
has turned the vines into luminous snakes.
I rub my forehead, feel the bones,
think of my own small mortal grin.
I lie listening as the future
rustles in the rhododendron brake.

LEAVEN

Though I think of words like archetype
and atavism
as I bake this bread,
rich, warm, smoky with corn,
I am silent.
This is a wordless ritual.
Yet I hear voices in a chorus saying,
"A pinch is just what you can hold
between two fingers."
I measure it now,
remembering the one who told me,
the one who told her.
Salt and meal, salt of tears and seas,
salt of the earth.
"Sweet milk will do, but buttermilk is better."
Their arms extend from rolled-up sleeves;
their faces waver as in Banquo's mirror,
a long line as they bend over hearths and ovens,
passing on the secrets of lard and leaven.
In a sizzling cast iron skillet,
batter hisses
soft as a whisper.

MONTGOMERY

Here by the river in the mist
of mock orange, Spanish moss and magnolia,
Southern clichés of humid days, warm rains,

the city sits,
dowager and debutante.
Here is the dignity of old homes and giant trees

and, at the fringes, golf courses in gentle swells,
a splash of interstate.
Downtown, Bell Street with its red brick

of public housing, mule-earred chairs on porches,
leads to Union Station. Dexter
slopes to the capitol's bronze star,

the Confederate flag still flying,
the fountain spraying mist and rainbows.
On Madison, farmers unload produce,

listen to their wives who bake, crochet,
grow gourds and collards.
Maids, returned from Chicago,

ride buses to Allendale, Thomas.
In winter bone-chilling rains swell the Alabama.
In summer, heat is a lotion,

oily on the skin and burning.
Air conditioners hum; sprinklers swirl
at the country club.

Here Scott and Zelda fluttered like tired moths
home to Mama Sayre and Felder.
Here King preached and Rosa Parks refused to move.

Montgomery sits as self-assured
as a grand dame at the D.A.R.,
fanning, sipping mint tea.

THE RADIO

Years and fears ago, at ten,
obsessed with spiders
and weak from a long illness,
I could not sleep,
for the world's dark corners
began in my room.
Spiders dangled from the bed springs.
That summer I had nearly died,
and the earth quaked under me.
A brisk, "Go to sleep.
There's nothing to be afraid of,"
left no comfort.
The darkness was darker still.

But there on the table
rested the Crosley,
dark and squat as a friendly troll.
Turned low, its golden glow
lit each corner,
and tall red tubes
peeped through the back.
Soft dance tunes brought in the world
beyond the windows where summer insects screamed.
Sleep came swathed in gold, dancing.

Yesterday you brought home a radio,
a reproduction, nearly like the one I had.
Because I told you.
Because you knew me.
How can I tell you this:
now in the night when the cold digital clock
and the dim green dial shed no warmth,
it doesn't matter.
I have accepted the spiders,
For, my darling, nothing is the same.
You anchor my world with light.

REMEMBERING ZELDA

Montgomery 1988

Two poets over coffee and crepes,
we sit in the converted splendor
of Union Station, conversing of another era,
words taking wing in stained-glass light.
You remember Zelda, tell how on the way to school
you crossed the street to avoid the witch
who wore layers of clothing.
I see you hurrying,
see the house half-hidden in wisteria,
a shadowy face behind sheer curtains.
Forty years under Maryland grass,
her body dust by now.
Strange what words can do.
Behind your head Scott and Zelda,
in camel's hair and cloche,
swirl through the doors.
Heels click on marble tile.
The steam from trains pants *hurry,*
while redcaps shoulder a path
through crowds and luggage.
Zelda pauses to light a cigarette,
stares straight into my eyes, and is gone.
I look beyond my lifted cup
at your animated face
and make a silent toast to friendship,
to Zelda, and to time.

THE BAPTIST LADIES TRAVEL TO THE FACTORY OUTLETS

To spend two hours by bus
(plus a stop at McDonald's)
they raffle apples and shout, "Apple time!"
then take turns telling jokes over the microphone.
Minds as sweet and blithely clean
as pinafores and shiny shoes, Bible schools ago,
they munch the apples,
while sun flickers through the windows,
and autumn trees seem to part in a swath, like seas.
Sisters in the Lord, pure lambs in polyester,
do you know we are traveling a landscape
where wolves raven and rage,
where doubt writhes at the core,
philosophy and physics
meet in mystical union,
and black holes suck in worlds?
Unscathed among lions and flames,
they glide over the highway,
talking discounts and coupons,
chapter and verse.
One whispers her secret
for perfect divinity. I listen.

YARD SALE

They gather in first light
before the dew has dried or long shadows
left the lawn, as silent in their greed
as insects feeding.
One thinks: "There's nothing here,"
another, "Over-priced,"
a third, "Just what I need."
The clothes, out of style or out-grown,
are piled in heaps on card tables.
The lady of the house, anxious but stone-faced,
watches the beetles clicking and picking.
After all, it is all "too good to throw away."
Ah, Thoreau, it's true that "When a man dies,
he kicks the dust." But now we cannot wait.
We pile our lives out on the lawn,
threadbare and confessional.

HESTER AND ARTHUR IN THE TWENTIETH CENTURY

Dimmesdale wears the letter now,
a signet ring with diamonds and rubies.
He and Hester have their own daytime show
and a house in Palm Springs.
Though she testifies sincerely,
some say his sermons are treacle.
Pearl and the Changelings shriek gospel songs
with a rock beat and subliminal messages.
Behind them a neon comet flashes.

By the baskets and by the month,
the multitude sends fish and barley loaves,
enough to open a Gospel Land
complete with rides and stage shows.
One wonders though
why Hester's mascaraed eyes are sad
and why she watches him so warily
as if he might fall from grace again.

Sometimes, she says, she misses New England's cold,
those soul-cleansing snows,
the deep, the austere, the grim.
Arthur only laughs
and gives her a boyish grin.

IT ISN'T POVERTY

and yet it is.
Stairwells that are urinals,
the sweet-sour stench of gin and vomit,
failure smells like these.

Sirens and screams,
a sick child's whine,
these are the songs of failure,
its voice.

Failure feels like dampness,
the fog that swirls through deserted train yards,
the dankness of dim alleys.

I've tasted it. The iron and lead of blood
and fear. It is mold and mildew in the mouth
and rancid grease, and it won't spit out.

Failure lives alone. It pulls the shades
and walks through dusty rooms, trailing rags,
avoiding mirrors. There is no phone.

HAWK ABOVE THE HIGHWAY

Hovering above the highway,
then perched on a telephone pole
between Hunter's Station and the river,
for a year now I have seen him often,
the hawk looking down on traffic
on blue fumes of exhaust and diesel,
his feathers ruffled in the wind,
head majestically turning in a half circle.
He should be sitting on a knight's gloved wrist,
be belled and hooded, then released
to soar over moor and heath
pursuing a helpless hare
or carved in hieroglyphs
upon some crumbling obelisk
close by the Nile,
but not here
between Kelly's Auto Parts
and the Western Club,
amid gas stations and cinder blocks,
above the rags of weeds along the ditches,
the wrappings and cans.
But there he is,
ancient Horus far from Thebes,
as alien as I.
Though invisible from here,
his eyes, I know, are banked fires
as he blinks in the morning sun.
He lifts to glide
in one low sweep across the road,
dips past my windshield,
then tilts upward to disappear
toward blue shadows of trees,
that distant world.

SUSURRUS

"*Susurrus*, a noun, or an adjective, *susurrus*,"
she explains. "Perhaps I can define it this way:
the Sunday dress when I was fifteen,
the way it slid between my fingers, all gold and green;
taffeta and crepe de Chine, and a velvet hat—
a kind of cloche really—black suede wedgies,
and hose from the drugstore, a dollar even then.
Lustre Creme shampoo…
do you remember that pearly sheen, the way it smelled?
Perhaps you wouldn't. You are too young.
Fresh and clean,
two lathers and a rinse in vinegar water
made your hair squeak,
fiery auburn drying in the sun.
The sound of the brush, the sound of taffeta.

"…*susurrus*. The whine of tires on wet streets
at midnight, hard with the glint of mica,
reflections of store windows, the lonely hiss
of tires moving away, the metronome
of windshield wipers
…or waking at night in the country,
listening through open windows
to the rustle of shock and fodder
beneath the harvest moon, or wind
in the cottonwoods, the patter the leaves make,
or the whisper of the river
slipping in shallows against muddy banks
beneath mimosas smelling of watermelon and rain.
How long has it been since I heard such silence,
knew such rest?"

"You must be able to use it in a sentence."
"Yes, I expect it will be on the test."

ELEMENTAL

I.
You are our home,
each separate grain of dark loam
our mother of the enfolding arms,
of flower and fruit, giver and taker.
Your granules heap at the root,
divide before the plow,
nourish weed and worm and owl.
Men die for you, lie in you,
become you, elemental as rock.

II.
The flow of it, isobars and currents,
the eagle and the condor held aloft
as they rest, wings spread, spiraling;
doors slam, and invisible fans
cool the neck, the brow, lift the laundry
on the line in billows. Flags snap.
Lungs fill with the essence of spirit,
light distilled.

III.
The flame's blue heart leaps
in candle or in coal,
wavers in elongated rings as in the tree's bole,
flickers like the serpent's tongue,
forked smoke of the snake moving like water,
the cold fire of ice and adder,
the opal's molten core,
black flame of spider.
The fire's dark center roars
and hisses, swells and diminishes,
smolders in organic combustion,
the slow sputtering of decay,
then splits the air with lightning
and is gone.

IV.
Rain-dollops roll in dust;
the air smells of mown lawn,
the green acridity of summer.
Rain plops like rocks in pools,
drenches the leaves, slides from the eaves,
pings on the patio, then slowly stops,
tapping on the trumpet vine.

Earth, air, fire, and water.
We drink this wine.

HANSEL AND GRETEL AT THE BEACH

Married fifty years,
they have dropped their years behind them
like a bread-crumb trail,
here where seagulls fight for crumbs.
Aged Hummel figurines in Bermuda shorts,
they stroll past the souvenir shops.
She, bowlegged, he, potbellied,
holding hands, they thread their way
through the crowds to the beach,
flat and swept, sand as gray
as dust from a vacuum cleaner.
At night the beach will be lit
by lights that dim the moon.

Seven stories up,
they cannot hear the sea.
Here they can forget
penny-pinching years, snow plows,
the string of shoe stores.
She writes the children in Larchmont;
he reads the news. They do not speak,
knowing in the deepest part of the forest
the witch waits in the gingerbread house.
But now they look at each other
across the king-size bed
and smile.

HARVEST

That green fruit, a bitter persimmon,
hard as our young bodies
in childhood and early marriage,
has become this ripe gold
I savor now,
a sweetness on my tongue.
I stand tonight alone in this autumn garden
and hear the locusts' undulating whirr,
a late bird's call.
A crescent moon hangs like a scythe in the tree.
How I wish you were here.
Only the breeze touches my hair.

PRODIGALS

Wary and visionary,
birds and butterflies take flight;
bees labor for late nectar,
and the ants, those misers, build hills.
The flash of Indian summer,
the burning pyrite,
affects these not at all,
nor my neighbors who rake and mulch,
light pilot lights,
stockpiling for Armageddon.

Only the cricket and I seem idle.
He sings in broken praise
of warm and endless days;
and I, writing,
search for wisps of words
evanescent as autumn air.
It will come; oh, it will come,
blackening and quenching,
sheathing the elms, the flowers.
But I hope the cricket will still be here.
If he is, I shall let him in
to sing the winter away.
And I?
A poem in my hand
will warm me
while the wind howls.

DAYS OF THE CRONE

Winter
is a spinster,
thin, with cold hands
and long fingers,
a Puritan who hates sin
except in her secret heart;
her tongue berates
with trees and wind
and whispers of innuendo.
All that is ripe and warm
she condemns with purplish lips,
pursed and hard.

I see her outside my window,
striding, black-shawled and bent,
stripping leaves from branches
for switches to sting
the legs of children
or brands to burn witches.

In the blackened garden,
she pauses to pray
for all that is lean and bare—
closed wombs, closed flowers,
the frozen ground in the graveyard;
for these she sings a hymn,
her voice cracked and tremulous.

Shivering in the snow,
she rattles her testament
and waits for revelation
as for a lover who never appears.

IT MUST HAVE BEEN IN AUTUMN

I.
These are the last sweet pressings,
the cider days, when wasps, sluggish and drunken,
hover above the windfalls,
and sulphur butterflies circle
on slow and lazy errands.
The morning air is piquant, spiced
with burning leaves, mulled
with woodsmoke and haze.
Cardinals, brighter than the dogwood's scarlet,
flash and dart,
and the last of the hummingbirds
sips from the trumpet vine.

II.
It must have been in autumn
when he tempted her,
whispered her name through the mist.
The jeweled fruit
must have rivaled the maple's red
and the garden been on fire.
She stood there wavering
and watched the clear streams
carry the leaves, spinning
them away beyond the boundaries
far to the east,
felt the restlessness that autumn brings,
a subtle stirring like leaves in rain.
She twined ivy in her hair
and then once more
she heard her name.

III.
If I could hold all of autumn in my hand,
I would bite the world like an apple,
listen to it crackle,
savor the winesap.
Oh, I would bruise this earth with my mouth
if I could hold this clear hour,
this air,
turning, burning with dying life,
the burning, burnished air
in all its apple-seeded richness,
tart and sweet and cold;
if I could hold one dust mote
of autumn's essence,
snatch one rounded molten moment
of this windfall day, this windfall light,
if I could hold all of autumn in my hand,
I would laugh and wipe the nectar from my chin,
then bite again.

STAR CHILDREN

> *Jim said the moon could'a' laid them....*
> —Mark Twain, *The Adventures of Huckleberry Finn*

Behind a cloud
or over the edge of the horizon,
the mysterious mating occurs,
some roving comet, no doubt,
fathering and moving on.

His progeny, tiny and throbbing,
are scattered across the Mississippi sky;
one, pushed from the nest, falls,
while all the star children look on.

In lapping waters
the moon
        drops
                feathers
                      of light.

OXFORDSHIRE

Summer Sunday noon and nothing stirs.
The street is funereal, a mortuary of heat
so still it seems coffined in layers
of bombazine, in tucks and pleats.
The sun reflects off asphalt and dull gray stones,
strikes the brass plates and the facades
where stability sits as rigid as Victoria.
The houses wear masks
as blank as a stranger's stare.
Trim boxwood gardens are colorless, harsh
with lines and shadows, and the fish in bordered pools
swim in slow flecks of fire;
nothing else moves.
Behind the lace curtains lives
are as closed as rolled umbrellas;
behind the lace curtains
dust settles.

CEREMONY OF NAMES

The field book rests next to the binoculars
because I am drawn obsessively
to label each bird at the feeder,
to question each wild flower,
what kind of tree, what kind of shrub
in a possession of knowing,
as if nothing exists
until given its proper appellation,
as if the naming were a source of power—
the shaman who needs your hair, the photographer
who steals your soul through your eyes—
or a need as old as Eden.

At sixteen in love with love,
breasts budding, and restless to grow,
I sat in biology class
copying dictation, countless phyla;
phylum after phylum rolled—
carnivores, herbivores,
mammals and crustaceans,
while outside spring waited
with its new unnamed leaves,
its pale aquarium light.
But the lists grew.
They elude me now,
students' names, the teacher's name.
Yet the need to know calls me still.

For instance, that tree,
is it honey locust?
What vine is that,
and that stalky flower?
And is that mullein,
thistle, clover, vetch?

To know, to know and so to own.
To know, to know and thus to hold.
Words in incantation roll,
and I call *crow, quartz, feldspar, agate,
walnut, cherry, wild verbena.*
Like God or Adam maybe
saying, "Leaf, you are important
and you are this.
I dub you moss, milkweed, ivy, tansy,"
and a whispered caress
gives each living thing
its living name.

STRAWBERRIE BANCKES

First Landing, 1607

Hearing the gentle breakers,
the sounds of birds in the mist and stillness,
we knew the land was there before we saw it.
After months of misery, many wept
or prayed in the lifting darkness.
Later, when we explored, the earth felt strange,
as if a cradle had stopped rocking.
The April sky was as blue and clean
as the fresh flowing streams,
and I was nearly ravished with the first sight,
weak with wonder at the scent of cedars,
the flowering meadows.
When someone called, we ran,
astounded to find the strawberries,
larger than any we had ever known.
To me they seemed a sign;
yet the wind blew cool off the Chesapeake,
and some shivered in the shadow of the pines.
Boarding again, a few looked longingly behind;
the rest of us faced the bow with hope
and wiped the juice from our hands—
blood-red as sacramental wine.

HOUSEHOLD ACCOUNTS

Monticello

I know the ironies better than anyone.
But there are practicalities.
Philosophy requires meat and drink.
I could live on air that sweetens this mountain,
but there are others to consider.
Bread is necessary and wine.
Perhaps out there where my telescope sweeps,
there is another way,
other worlds where ideals take form.
I know no other worlds, my heaven here.
Thus it is that I have achieved a vista
without cabins or quarters.
Only a few enter the dining room;
a dumbwaiter and a pivoting door
block the stench of sweat, speed the serving.
My guests are not offended or reminded.

Yet in my dreams they haunt me,
and she, Sally,
the odor of musk and copper,
the strong limbs, she who bore sons and daughters
I have allowed to wander away.
How can I deny freedom to my own?
So many have gone. Wythe, Hamilton,
friends and enemies, a wife, daughters.
She remains, substantial as bread,
heady as a wine I imbibe like a drunkard.

This minutia of journals has no end,
the household accounts, money and supplies doled out.
They give me pleasure, the sense of things well-ordered.
Yesterday the first poppies opened.

LESS THAN GREEK

Some days I don't think of you at all;
yesterday was one.
I prepared for the club,
got the teacups out and the china,
worked and cleaned.
Sixteen chattering ladies drowned out
the memory of your voice.
Someone read the definition of tragedy:
serious, complete, and of a certain magnitude.
Aristotle over cake.
Perhaps that is why I dreamed of you last night
wearing buskins and a mask,
while the chorus carried teacups
and chanted your name.
I awoke smiling from my sleep.
Our story was less than Greek.
Not counting dreams,
somedays I don't think of you at all.

NIGHT FISHING

> *I would drink deeper; fish in the sky...*
> —Thoreau

The moon trawls the sky,
      trailing a misty net filled with stars.
One star falls.

Beached by the tide, it lies
      on pale sand, dark, five-pointed,
cooling into stone.

I too would fling my nets,
      cast farther, deeper, to snare
the spendrift and spume of dreams,

draw in the spiny fins,
      then let them go to swim again,
flashing in moonlight.

Instead I stand on an arc of beach,
      mute and alone, the sky out of reach,
my lips cooling into stone.

HAUNTED

Warm in my car in winter light
I pass the house I read about
and feel the sinister pull,
the emanating evil.
Across the grass, across the asphalt,
through the steel,
something,

palpable, real,
dark, dark and hopeless.
Beneath metal awnings, the windows stare
like hooded eyes, half open.
Something stalks those halls.
I pass on, intent on driving,
thinking,

remembering the echo of laughter,
the gray ache of loss,
the sweet-sad phantom years.
Turning the corner,
wondering

if lost souls wander there,
I glimpse my eyes
in the mirror,
hooded, hurting, cold,
and behind them
fleeting shapes in shadows,
gliding.

TIME CAPSULE

to be opened on July 5, 2038

Fifty years into the future
as you open this, my unknown heirs,
my cloudy future seed,
think of the one from whom you came
and find the following:
two books of poetry;
a manuscript, unpublished;
thirty-three poems, uncollected;
three anthologies,
one short story,
two essays;
a journal of commonplaces, incomplete;
two photographs,
wire-rimmed spectacles,
two gold rings.
(The plain one is mine;
the other was my grandmother's.)
These I leave you,
the generations I shall never know,
but yet somehow I think I would recognize
freckles, dark hair, dimples,
a certain way of smiling, head tilted.
Now you are not in this world,
just as, when you open this, I shall not be.
Nevertheless, my children,
these small gifts are for you.
I greet you
and wave goodbye in love.

THE FOOD BEARERS

Even at the rocky crypts of Greece,
the wine poured upon the cairns
spoke of the sustenance grief must drink.
We have comforted with apples;
we have stayed with flagons.
Last week caught in the backwash of a wave
the vacationers never counted on,
a neighbor was taken by a heart attack.
Today his small son appeared with Tupperware.
I pointed him to the house where it belonged,
remembering other harvests never earned,
cornucopias burdensome in their plenty,
great platters of chicken, cakes, ham,
as if love could be heaped, ladled with gravy,
sympathy sliced, as if flour and butter
had hands or hearts.
We bear the offerings, accept the offerings,
understanding the braille of beets,
the mute calligraphy of beans.
We hear the onion's small *o*'s,
read the message of eggs,
feel bread's strong arm.

NEWSPAPER PHOTO, 1920

for my mother

The curve of the street,
the aqueous quality of light,
the thunderheaded sky—all are the same
though the buildings have changed,
brick by brick and stone by stone.
The dust is asphalt now,
and the livery stable's gone and the sycamores,
but it is still the court house square.

Blurred boys in knickers and girls in middies,
their bikes decorated for a race,
wait for the photographer.
One looks behind at someone else;
one shades his eyes.

It would have been your thirteenth year
and years before middle age
and three marriages.
You called it a movie star's life
without the screen.
It was over at fifty-four.

Horses neighing,
freckled hands gripping the handlebars,
sweat and heat and anticipation
must have made your heart race
on that hot summer day
before the race began.
I almost hear your laughter,
small and far away,
just as the shutter snaps,
freezing forever
the hope in your eyes.

A SEA JOURNEY

an elegy

In June twilight they are swimming
on the greensward of the courtyard
in the sea light of sinking sun,
a school of them
in long white dresses, in white tuxes,
aglow with their white teeth and healthy tans.
One by one as their names are called,
they stroke forward
to the speaker's stand and the rolled diplomas,
the beginning of a sea journey.

> In the Galapagos
> lumbering back to the beach
> where they were hatched,
> the sea turtles lay their eggs,
> prey to birds and the vagaries of a fate
> not cruel but indiscriminate.
> And the eggs hatch, most of them.
> Turtles as tiny as dimes
> bee-line toward the waves, the clear green
>   water,
> the cresting tops that slap them back and
>   back again;
> small legs paddle furiously, racing.

Now to the tune of "Pomp and Circumstance,"
we stand for the recessional.
I think of the years I have been here, the yearbooks,
the faces of those few lost forever.
The last off-key notes fade
as the sun sinks in a jubilee of pinks and golds,
reflecting gold in a swirl of white dresses.
The wind lilts in the trees
with a sound of rising waves.

NOVEMBER RAIN

Eyes alive with curiosity and fear,
ears alert and tail wagging,
he stood no taller than
the box we carried him in
the day we brought him home.
Years later we watched him,
arthritic and deaf, leaning as he stood,
gray fur in the wind, eyes like cloudy agates.
Before the city took him away,
I watched the rain rolling
from the plastic bag we had put him in,
heard a hollow sound like funeral drums.

This winter my father came,
sometimes walked about in the yard
on warm days,
unbent from his chair to change a channel,
talked endlessly of the past,
of riding horseback into mining towns,
trapping muskrats as a boy.
I lived it with him as he spoke,
admired the vigor of his mind.
But when he slept in the chair,
mouth open, hands unclasped,
I saw how frail he was and small,
and I shuddered,
hearing the November rain.

THE GENTLE WAY OF EARTH

The forest stump is lacy and splintery,
soggy with moss and riven by ants.
Conical as a small volcano or some troll castle,
it burns with a smokeless fire.
How long has this taken?
A hundred years, two hundred maybe
from seed to now,
and the whole forest the same,
alive with combustion, organic decay.
Giant trees lie awkwardly
fallen like dead lovers, one across the other.
Each thing sinks lower,
grows green and gray,
covered with lichen, fungi.
This is the earth's gentle way.

Our flesh goes quicker,
soft like the mushrooms
the ants devour.
Our spirit is the smokeless fire
of all we were,
though years may show in other faces
some nature that was ours,
or some word we said
may linger on the wind.
In a bit of forest sunlight,
pine seedlings rise
from the powdery needles of other pines.
From crumbs of earth
all things rise and fall
new and dying.

ABSENCE

No one would ever know
that a tree grew there.
From the east, light slants hard and hot
against my window,
glares where once the play
of limb and leafy shadow
softened the sunrise.
Neighbors' houses stare
into my privacy
with harsh outlines
of fence and brick and glass,
a view I never knew, till now.

It is like your going—
a brittle stretch of sky,
a slash of air,
the presence of absence
that cannot be defined.

FURNISHED TOMBS

Columbia and Victoria, how we ridiculed you—
you two old maids who, when your parents died,
bought a marble mausoleum
and furnished it for them—
with a lamp, organ, pictures in frames,
and at Christmas, a tree.
You wrapped the tomb with a big red plastic bow.
(The telephone company refused
to install a phone
that nobody was going to call.)
Oh, it was in the newspaper,
bow, lamp, pictures and all.
How we laughed,
peering through the iron grill.

That was twenty, thirty years ago.
Now I tend a grave,
bring flowers faithfully,
think of the pharaohs
sailing reed boats into eternity.

Columbia, Victoria, now I know.

FIRST FATHER'S DAY

Held down by a brown river-rock
on a bronze marker,
the card is faded by sun and rain.
Beneath the August sky in the sweep
of grass and plastic bouquets,
I read,
"To a great Dad, have a wonderful day."
and penciled beneath in a childish scrawl—
"I wish you were still alive....
Love, Shane."
Little friend,
I write poems, and if they were held down
by rocks and turned to the sun and wind,
still I believe I would write them,
just as you
send your penciled wish
singing into a void.
Words and love must go somewhere.
So I fling these words
along with yours.
Maybe someone hears.

NIGHT CRY

They come back to us in dreams,
and they never speak,
just as at the home razed years ago,
my grandmother is there exactly as I knew her.
Seeing her, I wonder if I am going to die.
When I ask, there is no answer.
My spoken words rouse me to remember
how in a dream long ago, my dead mother,
young and well, stood on a hill
and pointed toward green fields,
a distant stream, an orchard flowering.
Love was palpable.
Yet they are always silent, knowing.
It is we who, stunned, blurt out, stammer.

Sleep stretches into thick-tongued waking.
It is still night,
and the neighbor's dog is howling.
Forlorn yelps and barks waver
on rising notes of pain.
I wonder at that stricken call,
wonder at this world of gravity and graves,
where memory stirs like a restless child
and cries in dreams.

ANOTHER PICTURE

The shutter snaps as Wayne
stands among the Confederate dead,
looking down,
behind him a vista of greens and blues,
a valley wavering in the haze of heat,
thunderheads massing.
These beneath the upright slabs,
the clipped grass,
died as old men, one by one,
until there was no need
for the Confederate Home, now razed.
They were real as we are,
yet they seem representative,
only their names individual.
Today, picnickers come to read the names,
to see the view.

Our young friend climbs a chain link fence,
avoids its barbed top,
swings down on the other side.
Smiling, she shares the blackberries.
In my mind I snap another picture,
this one of the three of us now,
alive on this hill, laughing.
And I wish I could clasp time and hold it,
sweet and whole as sun-warmed berries,
wild blackberries
spilling summer on the tongue.
We help her across the fence again,
turn and wander
past rows of names, white slabs
where old men lie
beneath the Alabama sun.

GHOST STORY

Wandering lost, a ghost
glides over asphalt,
past gas pumps and car lots
where shade trees once grew
and the mossy sidewalk buckled
with their roots.
At an empty lot, he stops
at a trace of driveway,
stone steps, a tangle
of maples and mimosa
in a little glade
where a house had stood.

At his feathery touch,
loose mortar crumbles, whispering,
and the steps huddle
closer to earth.
Then, a child's laughter,
the screen door's wheeze and slam,
ice clinking in the glass,
and someone calling his name.
Now, only vines and trees and murmuring weeds,
and beyond, a susurrus of traffic.

Floating away like a gossamer strand,
his spirit caresses the ground.

GRACE

If Deity did not exist, still
I would thank nothingness,
though mindless, heartless,
for the unmerited favor of this day.
I remember my mother asking to be moved
so she could see,
her eyes swimming with wonder at a tree,
as if no tree had ever been before.
I know the speechless love she bore, dying,
for each living leaf.
That was thirty years ago.
Today the dazzle
from a drop of rain water
gathered in a begonia
blinds me with its strangeness.

For the benediction of rest,
the blessing of love's touch
and for tears,
for air's clarity, leaf's shine, the vine's
pale tendrils twisting,
for the dove at the feeder,
the nodding of his delicate head,
the squirrel with his paws clutched,
seed-full, like little hands in prayer,
for the corona of flame in the crow's eyes,
for teeming tenements in pond water,
amoeba, paramecium and tiny hydra,
for each living thing, wing and fin and claw,
I offer nothing but these simple words,
this brimming heart.

PERSPECTIVE, POWELL VALLEY

Next to a red barn waves
a field of cornflowers: bits
of sky on stems. Beyond, there
is a silo, and farther,
in a shallow swale, a spire,
delicate and white above red brick.
Then, fold-on-fold of blue,
the Cumberlands rise, cloud-crowned,
at the gap where Boone opened the wilderness.
Even then cornflowers, blue as faded denim,
blew in the wind sweeping down the mountains;
even then clouds dipped at twilight
and slipped pale fingers into the hollows,
cool and damp as graves of pioneers.

But that was then.
Now my heart is a beak
sharpened on granite.
In a hundred years these mountains
will lift their heads
and other eyes observe
blackbirds sleek as pokeberries
in summer rain.

III

South by Candlelight

HELD IN AMBER

circa 1947

A Sunday afternoon in summer's first heat,
the after-dinner bloat of ham hocks and greens
eased by slow rocking chairs.
No one hurries
except a dog scooting
under the town's one traffic light;
the unrepentant blink out of the theater,
duck into the drugstore's dim recesses redolent of
camphor and ice cream.
A car meanders around the square,
past the rotting bandstand
beneath the sycamores.
Later in the evening's yellow light,
children crack-the-whip,
end contorted as statues,
held in a spell
broken only by the first lightning bugs
rising from the lawns,
the sound of radios beyond dark screens.
It is a life colored in sepia,
twined with morning glories,
and no more real than some painted scene fading
on a moldering wall.
On Sunday summer afternoons
the jailer slapped his slattern wife;
cabs made bootleg runs.
Two blocks from the square, hogs
squealed in ramshackle pens
where bluebottle flies crawled on the swill.
Still, amber will preserve what amber will.

PERILS OF A SOUTHERN GOTHIC CHILDHOOD

Sometimes I wish I could leave
this quaking world and return
to that sweet time, but I recall
that nothing was safe—
insecurity lurked in the spidery pantry;
anger slammed the icebox door.
Mostly ignored, I listened.

Dinner times, having played too hard,
I sat exhausted,
the house hot with cooking,
nothing on the table a child would want—
runny greens, slick okra—
served up with stories of how people died.
Seeing Uncle Jesse lining up his peas,
Aunt Effie sopping up pot liquor,
I pushed the potatoes into pyramids,
played with my iced tea, drinking it
with the spoon jabbed nearby eye,
and listened to how someone fell
from a casket at a cemetery
and how they found him alive.

At night on the fern-filled porch,
folks rocked until the house cooled,
told scary tales of hants and prowlers.
The creaking, cooling house
dragged chains across my dreams.
At last Sunday came with hope and rain,
but a hell-fire sermon made me nervous.

I sang until my throat ached.
Then home to a crowded table
where grown-ups discussed sin,
named names.
Searching for the pulley bone,
I never missed a word,
until I remembered
the flopping death of the hen
now greasy on the platter.

Years later, troubled by strange fears,
strange dreams, exhausted from insomnia,
I recall only those I loved,
dim faces on a porch,
voices at a church,
and faces in a circle
around a dining room table.
The bed quakes under me,
and sleep is an open grave.

SKATE SONG

Whirring down the sidewalk
lickety-split,
I pass the Richardson's, Lou Ann's,
the pear tree, and listen
to my skates singing;
then I stop with a half-turn
and heel-to-heel turn again,
whirling up a dust cloud
that makes the zinnias bend backward.
I would be a bender of flowers,
a flinger of peonies,
a slayer of fences,
running my stick-stick-stick
along the pick-pick-pickets.

My skate key on its thong
bounces along as the wheels
make a needle of singing.
I am dizzy with summer,
the humming, bumping,
heat and speed, the wind
that balloons my sleeves.
Thirsty, legs trembling,
I skate on, thinking
of each crack, the sounds
my skates make breaking
my mother's back, the clack,
clack, clock of broken bones.

At last a dimming day
and a faint voice
call me toward home, the lure
of icy lemonade. Heavy as guilt,
skates drag in my hand
like some peddler's sack
filled with children
who never obey. He carries them
toward hills purpling
like a forgotten bruise.

NATIVITY ON ROOSEVELT STREET

At the Greater Macedonia Miracle Temple
it's Christmas eve,
and the windows are rattling.
The brethren and the sisters
shout and clap to the wail of trombones,
golden trumpets, the tambourines' tingle
and the thump of drums mingling
    with a chorus of
amens, hallelujahs, and oh yes, Lords.
Then Brother Lamar blots his forehead,
struggles with a fine point of doctrine
until he drops his thought
like a spool unraveling.
At his signal the piano breaks in,
pounds out "The Way to Glory,"
lifting the calendars on the wall:
Oh, yes, amen, that's the way.
Next door at Handy's Appliances,
a security light beams
above a chain link fence,
two Dobermans pacing.
Beyond the streetlight,
a small star shines, flashing
like a tear in Sister Emma's eyes,
as she beholds her son, two rows down,
home on parole, warm with food,
smiling at the music,
and safe for now.

NIGHT ON CRAIG MOUNTAIN

Smelling of deer hide and sweat,
tougher than raw leather,
they stalked like Indians through these hills,
cut trails through rhododendron brakes,
built fires against the wild-eyed night,
wrapped themselves in skins and slept,
callused hands close beside long rifles.

This was no Wordsworthian landscape,
daffodilled and idyllic.
The dreams that belonged to a privileged few
were left behind like winding streets
that curled past debtors' prisons.
What was here as they stalked these twisting trails
was not a dream for others. It was real,
something they could own.
Here loneliness was a salve, and black skies
beyond the trees burned with stars.

At night now on this mountain
cicadas' rusty screams rise
above a spring-fed creek;
only this ancient earth remembers
the soft pad of moccasined feet.

THE SORCERERS

The power to stop blood was never mine,
a power derived from Ezekiel and faith.
But others could. There were other granny women
out in the hills; one, born under a caul,
could cure "thrash." One had never seen
her father; another was a seventh daughter
of a seventh son.

Up muddy hollers and mountain roads
came families in pickups
or an occasional lone man on muleback.
Town doctors, though kindly, expected pay.
The fear of instruments, bottles and black bags,
the unknown, brought them here,
where nosebleeds stopped, sore mouths healed,
herb teas dried night sweats, and poulticed risings
drew to a head. No one laughed;
no one doubted the power of asafetida.

When I learned, years later, the secret
of "drawing" fire, I entered a sisterhood.
Even now, a lifetime away,
I feel a part of the rites
and the women,
women who could deliver a baby,
wring the necks of chickens,
then fix breakfast,
granny women, midwives, all
who fought pain
with incantations, with prayers, with teas.
Tonight there will be a full moon.
I hear crows caw.

THE LAST DRIVE-IN IN AMERICA CLOSES
Prattmont, May 1990

The performers have packed their trunks
and caught the midnight train
with all the troupers
who hoofed it from Peoria to Broadway
on a dime and a dream.
Where are Dan Dailey's straw boaters,
Betty Grable's spangled tights?
The Roxie, the Rialto, the Bijou
have turned off the lights;
they are as empty as jungle temples
where monkeys swing on vines.
In all the musty theaters
ghost voices linger,
mingle with the smell of popcorn,
the scratch of rats.

So now beneath the star-filled sky,
children sleep as family
cars snake out onto the four-lane;
their parents make mute good-byes.
The passenger pigeon,
the tiny snail darter,
Madagascar's lemurs—
other species have vanished,
just as metal speakers squawk
into silence,
pulled loose for souvenirs.

Above the concession stand,
above the empty spaces,
the patched screen looms
pale and monolithic,
a blind god's eye;
while in the field beyond
kudzu moves in moonlight.

FRESH LAUNDRY

The way the sun came through the windows, through
organdy bleached white,
and how sun came through the front door,
beginning to make its way
into the shadowed, summer-warm house,
and how we had no ironing board
and instead placed a long covered
plank between chair and table
and one-by-one removed the dampened mounds
of clothes—shirts, pants, skirts,
and pillowcases—the sizzle of spit
on the iron to test the heat or a dampened finger
gingerly dabbing, and the smell of starch
and bluing, the slick way the iron
would slide or stick, and the ache
of muscles—legs, back, wrist—
and how I sang
and daydreamed my way,
running the iron around a cuff or button,
flattening rickrack, a stubborn collar—
all these return on this spring day
as I remember how sunlight smells on cotton
and how wind whips sheets on the line.
Dirt and dinge are strangely gone,
stains of grief and pain,
rinsed away by forgiving years,
almost like April hanging out dogwood
and beginning again.

LOST TROVE: Appalachia

South by candlelight
and memory, take three paces west
and sight along
a rocky field
down to the river,
then around the river's bend
to the mouth of an abandoned mine,
along a line
pointing east
jut where three stars
rise over an Indian mound,
then west again.
See that furrow
made by wagon wheels?
Follow it two hundred years
to Carolina,
up a plank to a creaking ship.
Sail east.
Take cobbled streets
to a debtors' prison.
Wrap yourself in a ragged cloak;
wend your way
past winter fields,
hedgerows, sheep,
to a hovel, an empty dish,
a grate of smoldering peat.
When earth burns,
you know you're at home.
Dig here.

AFTER A LONG ABSENCE

Memory is a candle that won't blow out.
Though there is nothing here, new shoots sprout
where the maples stood,
and I recall

the odor of must and coal dust, and a two A.M.
　　train,
a dim bulb at the depot wavering in rain,
a ride home in Sim's truck
through the silent town, then Grandma letting
　　us in,

the ironstead bed smelling of camphor, old quilts
warm as a welcome, and the sound of wind
shaking the maples, rain on the screens,
then sleep, contented and deep.

Now, a few bricks, broken steps,
bring back all that is gone,
all that will never go—
maples and rain, the sound of wind,

life that ends like a long journey,
a sleep, and waking at home.

MOUNTAIN FOG

This is loneliness,
that air my great-grandmother said
would kill. I remember how
she shut the windows tight, no matter
the weather, to keep out the poisonous
dank, dark graveyard-air, the witches' breath.
And at night in those mountains it came:

heavy, wet, punctual, bringing quinsy, asthma,
those strange, thin fingers probing for death.
Last year I felt it again, cold at the bones,
watching it early before the sun had set,
creeping down the ridges, billowing, gray,
like a huge slow-moving flock of sheep,
and across the way the carillon

pealing out, "Oh, How I Love Jesus,"
mournful as memory and guilt.
As if the bells had called them,
the lambs came from every meadow, slowly,
inexorably, toward the helpless town,
while I stood there chilled in a dread
no quilt or window could ever shut out.

A GIFT OF POTATOES

After grace, I burst out,
"I'm tired of potatoes."
Her voice was surprised, low,
"I only fixed them because
I thought you liked them."
I poured catsup and looked away,
forked the salty wedges
waiting for them to cool.
She was too old.
My resentment curled like steam
that rose from bowls
and had no more words
than a sulking child.

The skillet had wrenched her wrists
as she juggled it to the stove,
dropped in the lard.
Potatoes, already rinsed
in water painful to arthritic hands,
slipped splattering
into the cast iron skillet
where they floated, bubble-covered,
roiling into gold.
And she, never hungry herself,
scooped them smoking
and steaming onto the platter
while I dawdled at the door,
winded from my noon walk from school,
hating the dangling light bulbs,
the linoleum with its black backing,
the backwater of living with grandparents.

When was it,
the day I realized
what it meant to cook
every day, only for love?

I imagine myself a child again,
and she is standing there
in the kitchen,
waiting, glad to see me.
I almost feel her small shoulders
as I whisper words not lost forever,

Thank you
for the fried potatoes.

A HOUSE BEYOND REPAIR

They both went slowly and together,
for there was never enough
to keep up appearances,
the gas-streaked, coal-streaked walls,
the decaying stairs.
Always something needed mending.
"And myself too,"
my grandmother laughed.
Though twenty years a widow,
eighty years had left her cheerful.

Perhaps it was a little draft that moved
the curtains and the candle flame
that brought her to stand last night
bow-legged before the fire,
hem lifted to reveal
the long-legged old-lady drawers,
hands spread to warm
the small, flat behind.
Framed against the light,
she was a scaffolding of shadows.

Tonight seeing the candle waver,
I thought about houses,
how when they get beyond repair
nothing can keep out cold or rain;
vines creep in and years.
Shivering, I remembered
childhood's shudders,
how she used to say,
"Footsteps on your grave."

APRIL REUNION

This is picnic weather.
The changing light on a begonia leaf
moves in molten slowness;
a quivering squirrel scallops his way
across a limb, stops to taste the bark
and scratches a flea.
A bobwhite name-drops hours on end.
Barnie paces the fence,
whines for me to play.
Birds bank against the sky.
Oh, I shall go mad with this;
never has a day been so blue, so green;
heaven's left its door ajar,
and the air whispers names:
daughter, mother, grandmother, cousins, all.

Today we shall have a reunion,
hearing together the songbirds, watching
a spider weaving and the ant foraging.
We shall picnic here on this porch.
Do you remember Walker Park,
that time we left the basket behind?
Do you remember Copper Harbor,
the cold water, the shining stones?
Water is a kind of curtain, too,
like this one, no more than a shimmer of green
between worlds. Remember how the water felt?
An ache of cold, slapping us around the ankles.
Grandmother tells me to settle down,
nips a dead leaf from a fern.

WATERMELON MOON

I.
To the country boy, all appetite,
hungry for a wider world than hills,
it was a watermelon, summer's last,
its shadowy center, a red, meaty heart.
His own was lonesome as the pale, empty sky.

II.
Through his window, the old man watched it,
and it caught like a lozenge in his throat,
bitter beyond swallowing.
How long had it been since he had heard
deep-throated bays, seen the raccoon
staring down and the moon through branches?
Remembering, he slept, hearing again
the cornstalks whispering in a field
of stirring crickets, his blood
and all of autumn making their music,
the yellow grapes, full with summer, swaying.

III.
The book closed, glasses put away,
she wound the clock and paused,
seeing there beyond the drapes
a scimitar, molten bronze;
she recalled Aladdin,
a world where wishes were fulfilled,
people stepped from pages, carpets floated
like clouds silvering the sky.

IV.
Caught between two buildings that way,
it reminded her of a Macy's balloon.
Once it would have mattered, been a sign.
Once she would have wished on it, another lie.
Rust flaked from the fire escape. Heat rose
from below. Her match flared, smelling of sulphur.
Now the tethered moon entered her blood
until something stirred like memory, bringing
a breath of air, the sound of wings,
home and a slice of watermelon moon.

THE SOURCE

Find again
mountains folding
blue-on-slate-on-blue,
thunderheads piling
anvils high as
the eye can see,
a stream that sings
tunelessly
and never stops
to change a note or stay.

You can rest here,
knowing that in every tree
your name is carved.
The earth gives to your feet;
the wind calls your name.
These rocks
formed to fit
the palm of your hand
warm now to your touch.

This is the place
that chose you.
When you arrive,
something opens
like the hinges of a door
long-closed and forgotten,
and a voice
you've always known
whispers, *Come in.*
You are home.

A SCENT OF GREEN

In a smothering haze of heat
the chinaberry droops.
Darkness gathers in the south,
and birds bathe in the dust.

A distant rumble; then a freshening wind
sets the wind chimes clanging,
cracks the laundry on the line.
The first drops spatter the leaves,
hissing on the cistern,
steaming on the roof.

The chinaberry writhes and bends,
slows to a stop,
as a steady rain
sends up a scent of green,
fecund and warm.

It rains till dusk
when fireflies rise from the lawn
and night birds call from the dripping trees
Clean   clean   clean.

ALCHEMY

Leaning on a blackbird's wing
to assay gold
and holding colloquy
with the beetle's fire,
the daisy jostles
the wall that hems it in.
The wind above its head
drops threads of milkweed
and slivers of light
into the caldron
of the daisy's eye.
Sorcery of summer days
alloys the leaves
of every tree and gilds
the lily and the lark.
Wizardry of summer nights
drapes the threadbare dandelion
nodding by the road and cloaks
the mud-faced toad in pearl.

DANGERS PAST

Red birds perch in the rhododendrons
and chime the minutes,
their calls like rusty bells.
A swallowtail alights,
then moves for a monarch.
The cat sleeps in a chair
but flicks his tail.
On the porch and under the screen,
a ring-necked snake slides and flows,
curls down under a rocker
and rests, a bracelet of small bones,
no more than a string of beads.
Then he glides away
like a question unanswered,
unaware of dangers past.
It is so still
I hear in the distance
the clock
the stream unwinds.

INDIAN SUMMER

near Cumberland Gap

I.
The yellow elm upon the hill
is burning still,
and every glowing bush returns
in ritual blood and fire,
an offering on the altar
of a dying year.
We should hear our names
in scarlet flames of maple, poplar, alder;
instead, we hear the shift of embers,
observe the flash of pyracantha,
leaf mold ankle-deep as ash,
and a light that shines like amber.
Only the breath of a falling leaf
whispers in the smoky air.

II.
Not far above, the highway winds
with its faint and distant hum,
but here a mountain stream
thrums over rocks.
Once Cherokees, hunting,
followed this narrow trail.
Perhaps one rested on this boulder,
took off his moccasins,
removed a tiny stone,
listened to the roar of water.
These rocks are worn, ground by years,
just as time grinds everything away,
and yet we make a path
to show the way we came.

Clean and swift, colder than death,
the icy spring pours
from the heart of the mountain,
bearing the leaves, small canoes.

III.
In moonlight two birds call:
"Here I am; here I am.
Where are you?"
Vines loop down like garlands,
 swing softly in the wind.
The air is cedar-scented.
Above these ancient trees
 dark skies string
the shining wampum of the night,
far-flung stars that form
a warrior's outline,
his bow poised always,
aiming toward the moon.

CARAPACE

> *...nymphs will drop to the ground and
> enter the soil to feed until the year 2,000.*
> —from a newspaper filler

The locust's amber skin
moves in the wind
as if alive,
but the locust has flown
to mate and die, its song
the signature of summer.

In darkness quietly stirring,
waiting through the years,
the nymphs will come again
to struggle toward the light,
to fly and sing
of cycles and of summer,

I may not be here then
to see the locust's shining shell,
to feel the autumn coming on;
yet I shall leave behind
a tatter of song,
an empty shell, when I have flown.

LIBATION

A cold wind knocks
upon the heart and scatters ashes
on the floor.
Autumn, let us bolt the door.
I have not sewn my shroud
nor canned the last rich store
of fruit, nor have you dried the sedge
nor bronzed the maple by the pond
nor turned the berries brown.

Instead we sip sauterne,
hold it to catch the light
of setting sun and taste
the drops upon our tongue.
Let us toast the wasted hours,
the scattered flowers,
then spill this wine
upon the hearth where no fire glows.
For someone has told the sexton.
Hear the bells.
They are tolling summer down.

Autumn, we will twine and plait our hair,
chanting with the last slow bees
litanies of frost.
The roses are wearing golden crowns,
and doves are mourning
with the bells tolling summer down.

FALLOW

Weeds push their stalks here,
thistles, Queen Anne's lace,
ten million million wildflowers;
rabbits stop and twitch and browse
where a house once stood
now fallen into rubble,
a barrow empty of chalky bones,
and, against the bank,
a spring house, stones tumbled,
a kind of monument to apples
and survival. Once there was a view,
a lake, gone now, only the plain
of it remaining in the far meadow.
Stillness settles like heat
and muffled thunder.
Nothing is restless but the wind
clicking beads and saying its prayers
and a butterfly flicking its way
somewhere.

MAGNOLIAS

Leaves talk when women
lean over the pasture fence
and watch their children
herding cattle home,
and a small, self-important dog
yips ahead.
Cowbells swing slowly
in time to the lowing,
clanging and fading,
then clanging again.

Redolent of powdered skin,
crinoline, lace, a memory
of plenty, lime-sweet flowers,
big as bonnets, whiter than porcelain,
move in the wind.

Blossoms are a solace to tired women
knowing chores are over
and evening waits
with clean sheets and a turned-down bed;
but now they pause
in the fading light of a worn sun.

Stamens yellow with pollen
make candles to light their way
as tongues of leaves
whisper the women home.

ON BUYING A SPRIG OF QUINCE

Oh, I say,
seeing it there,
among the turnips,
the kindling, and cakes,
and I say its name
—quince—
feeling it, faintly citric,
tart, cold and hot,
like spring:
breath and juice,
all in a sound.
The farmer lifts it
dripping from a bucket,
hands it to me,
stem wrapped and wet,
coral blossoms and bare branches
forming a calligraphy
as subtle as the Orient.
I carry it, prickling,
catching on everything,
through the dark market
and into February sun.
Now in the porcelain vase,
the one where the sea-serpent
coils, gold and undulant,
ragged blooms gather the light
of dying winter. The sun crawls
like a serpent toward spring,
spreading dragon-flames,
smoky tongues of flowers to come,
like quince—this blossoming stone—
or spires of larkspur or the iris's
blue bruise.

ONLY THE LOCUSTS

The locusts are lamenting,
their wavering notes
rising in the cooling air,
an organ fugue, melancholy and endless.
They tell us summer has passed.
See where she has trailed her silken gown?
There are faint silver streaks
in the long grass
where the last of the fireflies
flickers alone and rises like mist.
What summons has signaled
the hummingbirds?

They no longer come,
having darted to the Yucatan.
In the absence of their wings,
the kamikaze wars,
only the locusts hum,
and among the withering vines
a star or a firefly shines.
Ghost of a dying year,
I await your return,
certain of your love,
silent as a bulb.

SNAKE

Suddenly there at my feet,
then squirming sidewise away,
the small gray snake
disappears like a dream of smoke,
under the dripping edge of the creek bank,
leaving me numbly aware
that he is afraid of me.
Having just molted,
he is unidentifiable, somehow pup-like,
vulnerably clean.
And last night on my wall, a gray millipede
big as a feather.
When I turned for the spray,
he was gone.
Yesterday the quick rabbit in the road
ran with his small pounding heart
ready to explode. That rabbit has my heart.
The moth at the window, slapping at the screen,
we are one. Fearing the surgeon's
    knife, the lance,
the dark, the spray, the needle, the gun,
we may step away, run, hope for mercy,
hope for speed. Or pray.
But all, all are the same.
Man and moth and millipede
and small gray snake.

MOUNTAIN BATTLE

The sourwoods are the first to know
that fall is marching south.
The army travels quietly;
the horses' hooves, felt-shod;
then a hint of red among the apple leaves
shouts the alarm. Maples bugle reveille
with notes of brass and bronze.
And soon the battlers clash
with sword and grapeshot rattle.
Sumacs flash; cattails drum;
vermillion crashes through the woods,
sets the brush aflame, leaving
smoke above the ridges
and haze above the pond.
One cicada sounds retreat,
but far too late. A cold wind
blows a pod against the barn;
red leaves are floating on the river.
Toward the valleys south of us,
the massacre moves on.

(I saved the dogwood berries.
I saved some silver in the well.
I'll show you when the moon is full,
and the wind is still.)

SPRING RAIN

Wisdom should speak slowly
and softly, like rain maybe,
that thin spring kind
that filters down through the leaves,
that drips from the eaves,
that misty, long-lasting kind
that sets in for the day,
and you know how everything
is drinking it up;
wisdom should be like that, gentle,
talking slowly and softly.

LOVE AND A SEASON

Reluctant as a yellow leaf
that won't let go,
my autumn grief at last
has flown, leaving in its place
a quiet peace
that settles like snow.

How frantic was the spring,
offering bouquets,
jonquils and quince,
forsythia's dripping branch,
making foolish promises
of endless green.

Lazy summer settled,
content to stay
as long as hummingbirds
and phlox, as long as weeds
along the way, then faded
into letters moldering in sachet.

Nothing could survive the cold,
not one aster, not one bee.
Frost flowers upon the pane
etched their mockery.

The moon is small tonight,
pale as a flake of drifting snow,
and around this barren room, wind
like a lost soul, seeks its own,
but, darling, I recall
that burning spring,
the ripening,
the summer, and the fall.

WINTERSCAPE

for two voices

Warmed by ocher,
umber, ecru, sienna, sepia,
Alabama pastures are backlit
by sunrise, misted by fog.

> One can hear strands of song,
> as if time forgot to close the door.
> *Mary, don't you weep. Poor little Jesus boy.*

In a grove beyond,
a thin skin of water,
left by rain, mirrors
dark trees, moss hung.

> Another Cain, hunting deer,
> killed his brother, and there is the tree
> where they say a runaway swung.

Overhead a stain of peach
and mauve, rimmed by gold,
holds blue pools and a paling moon.

> Smoke lingers from the stir-off.
> Last night's moon was sorghum-gold.
> The river's scent and sweet grass blend.

A slash of pines,
cedar, spruce
stand tangled
in a snarl of vines,
and in the distance a barn
sags red with sun.

My father's hands are cracked like pine;
his knuckles are burls. When the calf died,
he held it and cried like a girl.

The hayfields are alive, afire;
burnt-orange spreads
to meet the sky.
Down by the pond,
white egrets flicker,
lost in landscape, light.

TAO

> *It is... the abyss that was before the Creator himself.
> It is the Way the universe goes on.*
> —C.S. Lewis

The voice without a voice
whispers
the way a rain cloud
catches on a mountain,
dipping down and then
flowing over,
strand on tattered strand;
the way lichens clasp the oak,
little gray-green shelves,
frilled and brittle;
the way kudzu wraps
itself pole by pole,
then hides its blooms;
the way mushrooms make red explosions,
the way the spring seeks its way
between the ferns,
and the way love and pain
return, endure,
seasonal, unchanging.
Something flame-like, pure,
throws out filaments
that reach and climb
like a spiraling hawk,
a twisting vine;
more than wind
ruffles leaf or water.
Stand in the midst.
Listen.

FOOL'S GOLD

Only a fool could find value here:
joy in the lily's dusty throat, the laden head
bending toward the bee, the wind that sways
coreopsis, sorrel, and rue;
joy in a quivering mouse hunched in his hole,
joy in the serpent's black coils
gliding over sun-warmed rock,
the cat crouched in tall grass,
the electric ripple of fur and muscle;
joy in hawk and owl, in seed and weed,
in wings and fins, in all that darts
and swims in water, in air: the dazzle
of minnows, their skittish dance;
the frog's bassoon, the flute of wood thrush,
the piccolo of wren; joy in water, in wind,
joy in every blind, groping thing:
the bat, the burrowing mole, the worm;
joy fleeting as innocence,
fool's gold, worthless
in the face of despair,
coin of the silly, improvident poor;
bright cheap toy, coin of my realm.

TO A FERTILIZER SALESMAN FROM LAUREL, MISSISSIPPI

Orchards ago,
your name forgotten,
I remember that summer
of sand and forbidden fruit.

Following me when out of view
of your hawk-eyed wife,
taking walks when I did,
you finally stopped me,
and I stood listening.
"If you're ever in Laurel, Mississippi…"
I did not reply, though my eyes may have.
The fruit was dew-covered and within my reach.

Next day, far up the beach,
silhouetted by the rising sun,
a bronzed Burt Lancaster, towel in hand,
you waited for our expected rendezvous.
Oh, I was hungry for fruit,
but I turned on Deborah Kerr feet,
tasting the tartness on my tongue,
never knowing what I refused.

Orchards ago,
your name forgotten,
yet dear fertilizer salesman
from Laurel, Mississippi,
wherever you are, whoever you are,
it might have been sweet.

THE BAPTIST LADIES MEET AT QUINCY'S

Over cream of broccoli and over salad,
we bow for the blessing,
then put aside pleasantries
as anxious whispers rise.
Scandals have increased attendance;
a deacon faces jail,
and the pastor's days are numbered.
David phones Bathsheba
anonymously and repeatedly,
and Lot's neighbors
are pounding at the door.
Armageddon hovers
closer than the waitress
who refills our tea.
Nibbling at scandals of the past,
the stale crumbs
of business meetings and power cliques,
we pass crusty rolls shaped like stones
while our faces waver in night-dark glass.
Later we continue talking outside
oblivious to the damp air
heavy with the effluvium
of the paper mill, the stench
of steak and brimstone.

THE CHEERLEADER

Cotton candy girl,
made of spun sugar and air,
you sit on the second row
in your cheerleader's uniform
and tee hee your way through *Macbeth*.
My scathing look could ignite asbestos,
but you open your compact and check your
    beaded lashes,
unaware of a world beyond your reflection.

When I call on you,
your vacuous eyes,
empty as Orphan Annie's,
dart around the room.
Then you open your peach-frosted lips,
snap them closed,
as if you thought better of your reply.
Galahad on a white charger blurts
    out an answer,
receives a dazzling and expensive,
orthodontist's smile.

Child, I think of your future,
wonder if ambition, guilt, tragedy,
will ever touch you.
Perhaps at thirty you will discard husbands
like lipstick-blotted tissue,
or they will drop you.
Perhaps the years will put character
on that porcelain mask,
blow away the froth and fakery,
or find you just as silly, only older.

Macbeth addresses the candle.
You giggle again.

ON MEETING A CHAMELEON IN MY MEDICINE CABINET

We were both shocked;
I, reaching for the Tylenol,
and you, red-faced like the cap, blushing.
If a lizard can travel through my winter house
to greet me in such a way,
then why not say embarrassed?

But most of all I think
I was stunned at your eyes,
the curiosity that flashed, the way you tilted
your bean-sized head and stared
as if you knew me,
had even perhaps known me before
in a kind of lizard déja vu.
And your little eyes, sharper, brighter,
quicker than mine, asking a question.

Pragmatic, I took a tissue, wrapped you in it,
and carried you through the den,
dropped you once,
alarmed at how fast you scuttled away; then I
caught you again, and out the back door.
But I was left wondering. I am yet.
Ah, Horatio,
I remember those eyes.

INSTRUCTIONS

It's best to take it young,
but anytime will do.
Give it a life
stifling with details,
too many concerns
and the clock striking twelve
twenty-four hours a day.
Make sure it never sleeps,
at least not well.
Then provide friends,
the kind that move in
and stay and ask and ask and ask
and say but we need
we need we need.
When it dares to try,
present a critic or a dozen or two;
make it aware that for every choice
a million others would do.
Put it in concrete, pour on asphalt,
clipped grass. Never let it hear
a mountain stream, breathe clean air.
Do you see something green,
one little shoot, something trying
in dark to survive? Present a world
gone amuck—violence, cruelty,
and last remove the human ear,
whatever's left of heart.
Done. A talent dead.
Tomorrow our new world can start.

FIRST READER, POLITICALLY INCORRECT

Dick and Jane and Spot stand spotless
on their crisp page;
their white house gleams
beneath the stately elms.
Jane holds a sugar cookie;
Mother sets a table under the arbor;
Dick sips a frosty lemonade.
We children of the grubby hands,
the run-over shoes, we motherless,
fatherless waifs of air raids and rationing,
hold you in a memory too innocent for envy,
knowing you only as our first dream,
our first heaven.
Look! Look! See!
Even now, you are there,
alive in perpetual spring,
where Spot runs endlessly
beneath shadowy trees
and Jane calls, "Watch Spot run."
Someday if we work hard,
keep our crayons in the lines,
we will live on your street,
be your friends, use your shiny skates,
catch your bright red ball.

CAMELLIAS

I've never liked them,
blossoming out of season,
blemished or curled
or too perfect in some sickly way.
No, I've never liked them—
hypocrite flowers in "put on" frills,
overly virginal among waxy leaves,
out of place in winter, awkward afloat
in crystal bowls on mahogany buffets,
hinting always of tornado weather.
Without fragrance, without warmth,
they are society girls, proper as pumps
and white gloves and malicious remarks
worn with the proper pearls.
Cotton's dressed-up cousin
at a masked ball at Mardi Gras
or at home amidst the squalor of the blighted
neighborhoods or yellowed lace
and better days, they remain as they are
though dying at the core, stolidly present,
slightly unpleasant, like moss-draped trees
in graveyards where black snakes sun.
Ever-present as weeds among tombs,
camellias fester and bloom.

CONJUNCTIONS

"But" is the creaking hinge
the world swings on,
the cold air that breathes
from revolving doors.
The gift once freely given,
taken back again,
it is the lie the lover tells
when love ends.

"And" is the strata in canyon walls,
levels of meaning layered
in histories of shale,
the shadow of thought, winding in arroyos,
leaving an inky trail.

"Or" is the grinning troll
that shakes the midnight bed
with daytime choices remote as sleep
and real as dread.

"Nor" never picks its teeth,
nor trips over its feet,
nor behaves itself unseemly.
It never joins that commoner "either,"
being far too kingly.

"For" reasons and manipulates,
convinces and consoles;
the lawyer of language,
it explains and cajoles.

"Yet" is the pardoner,
the governor's midnight call,
the quiet fate that waits
before the blade falls.

A NIGHT OF BINGO, MOUNTAIN CITY, GEORGIA

It's Tuesday night and lonely;
there isn't much to do.
But few seem to socialize.
Though pickups fill the graveled lot,
the crowd is mostly women,
old and in athletic clothes;
a few men in overalls, baseball caps;
children, pale and well-behaved.
A cloud of smoke rises like incense,
prayers, dreams,
joins with mountain fog,
the monotone of katydids
drifting through wide doors.
Spreading out snacks, coffee,
we settle down for serious playing.
One by one the caller drawls the games—
picture frame, picnic table, postage stamp—
as tension rises.
Dabbing quickly with the daubers,
experts lean over, help amateurs.
New at this as well,
Gladys is sweetly senile,
needs too much help.
She reads a monitor aloud,
throws me off.
The jackpot is a cover all.
Two numbers away
I'm tired and want to quit.
It's got to be close,
any minute now. Come on. Come on.
Then, "Bingo!"
and like a mantra, sixty-three voices
intone, "Ah, sheee-it."

BUFFALO BILL AT THE PIGGLY WIGGLY

Don't tell me he's defunct.
Why I saw him yesterday
unwinding those long legs
out of a pickup truck in the parking lot,
all decked out in leather and fringe,
tight boots to his knees,
striding with a kind of rhythm
past the cart corral.
Lord, how good he looked,
white shirt next to that tan
and all that silver hair.
I've been younger,
but I've never been better,
and I ain't never been dead.
So he was a looker,
and I looked
at that hard-riding, lean
ol' buffalo man.
He slid through the doors,
rounded a pile of cantaloupes,
then vamoosed past the cabbages
and disappeared,
but I know he's somewhere out there
with a sack of groceries and a wicked grin,
long hair blowing in the wind,
riding the back roads of Georgia.
Buffalo Bill's still a blue-eyed man.

FEBRUARY, '63

for Sylvia Plath

Steam hisses across damp starch
that smells of earth, moldy.
A cotton-wool sky sheds lint.
The BBC discusses the worst winter
in a century; coal is short.
My hair in brush rollers,
I stop to smoke, sip coffee,
arch my aching back.
Slightly bored,
I listen to my children squabble,
test the iron with a wet finger
to make it sizzle,
words rising in my mind like steam,
vague wordless dreams waiting
like the poems I have yet to write.
But for now I sing a tuneless hum
and run the iron along a sleeve,
my happiness as fragile as lace.
Not far away a poet watches London snow,
listens to the tea kettle shriek
above the blue flames.
She thinks its voice her own,
that wavering fumes call her name.
The snow has slowed the trains.
The snow separates us. We are young.
We have children.
We will never meet.

NIGHT COLLEGE

I change an F to a D– and back to an F again,
pity and a mercy killing contending.
You hardly recognize a sentence.
Noun is as unknown as security.
There are no dreams in your face,
no sparks of thought or inquiry.
Just exhaustion.
One term cannot correct a lifetime.
I cannot. And here is your paper;
your chosen topic, spouse abuse.
I know you know.
Finally, the F remains,
a scarlet letter blazing in ball-point,
trumpeting my guilt.
I read your paper again.
Your tired black eyes stare at me
from every line
until I hang my head, Pilate with a pen.

TRAVELERS

Despair and fatigue travel together.
Neither believes in dawn or gods;
they plod but leave no footprints
in the slush of snow.
Around them black dots of soot
settle slowly.

Aged and wizened, they breathe
asthmatic breaths; their skin
has the pallor of ash
and carries the stench
of cabbage and gin.

They are the rag and bone men
who pick through garbage cans
down alleys where only rats
grow fat, and darkness comes on
like sick-bed sweat.

Beneath street lamps
where poisonous fog
wraps entrails of gray,
they make their way
toward the yielding bed
of the hopeless heart.

GENESIS

They had to go,
dusty and utilitarian
with wasps and rolypolies
dangling and spinning,
and the spider rappelling down his wire.
So one hot morning the broom fell,
and a kingdom was gone,
all that geometry a chaos,
and bugs scattered like planets.
The porch gleamed, swept clean,
but, still, it seemed wanton,
so arbitrarily mean.

I've been there: through far too much,
having seen earth cover the best
I could construct. I know how much
it costs to lose a universe.
Perhaps that is why
when I saw today the gleam
of a leg weaving and flashing,
when I saw bright filaments
on fire with a dawning sun,
I wanted to applaud,
knowing how hard it is
when a world ends
and is begun.

GOOD WATER

Good water, cold and clean,
wind off snow,
the sound of a mountain stream
chuckling over stones,
light through leaves,
maple's flame—
all these
in syllables' sibilant hiss
or vowels round and slow—
the moan of *ohs*—
the lightest touch of the lightest kiss
or the dying screams
of those in pain,
heart's blood, spring rain,
the poem winds its
sinuous way,
saying what we cannot say
or name,
bringing that taste of earth
from a deep wellspring,
this good water, cold and clean.

POETRY TEACHER

Speaking the sibilant syllables,
the magnificent thunder of vowels,
whispering and crooning my cadences,
I cast my spell.
Some escaped,
closing their ears, sealing their souls;
there are always a few who escape.
But not you.
When I saw the answering fire in your eyes,
read your singing lines, I knew.

Now, my child,
you will gather mandrake by moonlight;
in the black caldron of time,
you will brew the timeless potion.
A demon at your heels pursuing,
you will ride through this world
and never be part of it.
Cursed and blessed,
touched by this cold light,
searching always for the dark roots
beneath the surface of things,
you will never be satisfied or filled.

For into the future...I see you,
wrapped in mist,
your coat flapping in the wind
the wild light in your eyes....

Child, you have joined this coven.
You are mine.

Remember your teacher
who cackled these words to you.

FACING THE AUDIENCE

Pale as fungi, the old poet reads,
expert in modulation, the rise and fall
of lingering syllables that say,
"This, in case you doubt, is poetry."
He has always been, to quote a phrase,
in love with death.
Now terminal but with eyes
acutely alive, he sparkles
with humor and vanity,
rather like Frost,
though without the honors.
And it all comes down to this:
awed students, the better ones,
alert to puns and nuances,
the subtle symbols,
and the older group aware
of their own advancing years. Death, too,
slumps in a chair, not bothering to applaud,
bored, but infinitely patient.
(A bat wavers in and out of the room.
Someone closes a door.)
Caressing his dying,
he reads so well one can almost forget
his throat wobbling, the pallor.
If pain ennobled, such suffering
would have meaning, a bleak-eyed audience
could find some comfort in his valor,
his waving hands that emphasize a line.

Their minds are not always there;
some are thinking of work,
the hardness of the seats,
the petty vermin-voice of worry.
He turns the page,
and in the cool night air
beyond the auditorium, stars wheel,
blink on and out.

TONGUES OF FLAME

Spring rain and darkness
impel me to light a candle
and listen to Callas.
The flame's dusty halo
and a rising melody blend their gold,
And then out there, glad for rain,
a mockingbird gone insane
and perched somewhere under the eaves
trills every song he knows,
telling secrets of green twigs stirring,
while death, hidden in shadows,
folds its wings.
Notes cascade; notes rise,
in tongues untranslatable:
glossolalia of bird, soprano, rain,
and the candle's small lilting sun.

THE LOVERS

All lovers know,
taste it like salt of the sea,
and hear the sound of a clanging gate;
but in a rented flat
seven stories above the street,
they imagine it again.
When it returns, the earth shines
like mica in a mountain spring,
and blade by blade new grass spreads
across a plain where a man and a woman stride
naked as green bark peeled.
At evening, she bakes bread
on a rock by a shining stream;
they savor root and herb,
and all night make love under the stars,
wound in each other's arms.
Under their heads the sun-warmed sand
yields to arm and breast.
A light rain through the leaves
touches thigh and lash,
but they only turn and sigh.
Nothing owns them or harms them.
Nothing but time.
When daylight comes, they wake
to a seedy flat, sun on a tattered shade.
The baby cries, then finds his toes
and laughs. Before they rise,
their hands meet
across tumbled sheets.

COLD COMFORT

Hollow as a sieve and empty now
of all that mattered,
the house had corners
space heaters could not reach,
nor would overheating compensate.
Air that hovered above linoleum
wrapped its cold breath around her feet.
Beyond the steam at the windows,
beyond the glare of sun, brightness
dazzled. Snow again.
Peeping through lace, a winter bird
through evergreens, she knew
she must remain nested,
find what comfort walls could give.

Peaceful hours stretched endlessly,
unused as a ball of yarn, trackless snow.
The sound of the clock in the hall
boomed into her chest, became her heart.
The plate and cup she washed and put away,
took out the memories and dusted them
one-by-one, made the bed, watched TV,
talked to a friend on the phone, remembered,
remembered again.
In the mirror dim faces wavered,
their little voices squabbling,
"That's mine. Mama, make him give it back."
Hush, children, hush now, be still.
The house cracked, settled.

After supper she sat in darkness,
listened to house and wind.
Fire in the heater became a friendly eye.
In bed she stretched out her hand
to his side, an empty hollow,
the sheet cool, silky as skin.
From the eaves quietly,
the snow began its slow thaw,
melting like years.

PAGODA VILLAGE

an African ground cover

A forest floats in the sea
where jellyfish ballet;
life beneath the microscope
dances and darts;
the peacock's feathers
are a shimmer
of azure and eyes,
but observe this silly plant.
Its intricate origami
forms pagodas, stacked
and tilted as if on stilts.
It says more to me
than evangelists or prophets
who rarely smile.
What could they say of a joyous Creator
hurling comets and planets in play?
Crafting this plant
with a rolling belly-laugh,
He set it in the soil
next to the ostrich and giraffe.

CIRCLE OF LIGHT

The caption reads 100th birthday,
and he stands above a bonfire of candles,
holding out his hands to warm them.
No carbon of memory can resurrect
the passions burned away,
the corners curled and browned
where the calendar turned.
Outside the dungeon where we dwell,
he lives in the purity of the cautery,
that sealed off room, that clean scar,
of one who has survived
the fire that now burns from his eyes,
a pristine flame, more alive than we
who stand outside the golden ring,
still caught in these shadows of hours and days
and capture in black and white
a flash of living light
surrounded by darkness.

WIDOWS' WALK

Walking is their early ritual.
Avoiding city traffic,
they have made a path
around the cemetery,
past the veterans' monument,
the garden of prayer, past the chapel.
Some stop to chat, talk about weather,
trod on. The stones around them
are as familiar as faces; many of them
are names they have known.
Wiser than their worried children think,
they are aware of ironies,
see the dates of those plucked young,
wonder, wonder, trudge on.
They are not inured,
having lost so much themselves,
but they do not dwell on questions.
Instead, they think of breakfast,
plan their days, stop to listen
to a strange bird's call,
watch a cat slink from a hedge.
The sun is out, but a light rain
starts to fall. Their cars are waiting,
tea and toast, another day,
the telephone.

FEATHER IN THE WIND

In front of the church-house steps
a carnage of feathers attests
to nature's plan.
There is little left,
not bone or beak or claw.
And yet He knows each sparrow's fall.

He knows the cat or owl,
whatever preyed upon this lawn
and tore away one song;
whatever plan, whatever pain,
karma or providence
beyond the mind of man,
He knows it all.

I look at elm and sky,
a white spire overhead
and feel my own heart fluttering
and know a dread.
More than sparrows, He said,
more than lilies in the field.
I watch a feather in the wind
and turn away, not comforted.

NIGHT WATCH

In this sparse garden only shadows bloomed.
Nothing was green but mossy stones,
cedars, cypress, olive trees pale as the moon.
Even the moon rose gray as bone.
Yet earth was a vine that held him here,
strong as a rope these withes of love.

Perhaps as he prayed, a finger of wind
lifted his sleeve and touched his hair,
and perhaps he was aware of bells
from sheep and cattle, a herdsman
singing a song. Loving earth,
perhaps he remembered
hewn boards stacked in dusty air,
the plane and adze; fishing for perch,
their jeweled scales; grapes musty, splitting;
the rasp of grain in his hand,
sun on water, sun on crops;
his mother gathering herbs,
the way she studied him.

Loving earth, how could he not
be clasped by its green, the tendrils
of grass he rolled in as a boy?
The garden around him lay swathed in fog
and cold. But still he prayed
and strand by strand uncurled the vine
and let it go.

REMEMBRANCE

Far from Cana and from Galilee
miracles occur quietly.
One grain of corn
sown by wind or by man
increases and increases again;
multitudes are fed.

Far from Cana and from Galilee
miracles occur quietly.
The vine draws water through its roots
to swell the grapes;
sweetness and sun ferment
water into wine.

In the stillness of my thought,
I hear ancient words,
think of ancient agonies,
the dark mysteries of blood.
I hold in the miracle of my hand
this bread   this wine   this love.

SINGING WHERE WE ARE

The schoolyard sparrow
has made his nest of grass and cellophane,
a tenement where crepe paper uncurls.
Not far away the hummingbird
lines his nest with thistledown;
it is a swinging pillow.

Shadowed by mountains,
a palace for a robber baron
looms amidst vineyards,
and further south a chapel
cradles the remains of Dukes.

Only yesterday
under Vermont's gold maples,
Frost, flinty, crusty,
plotted and mumbled.
In Amherst, Dickinson burned away
her life in her father's house,
ticking off eternity in dashes.

Under mountains, under maples,
these homes, these little houses,
these whistling bones!
Birds and barons and bards, all
twig-builders, all weaving,
feathering nests, singing.

WHEN SPRING TOUCHED WITH FIRE

Little moves here but birds flying.
Stolid as the frozen ground are those who wait,
here in this clarity of cold,
white-on-white and blue,
black trees, the granary standing empty,
its door open to the wind,
nor can they remember the frozen lake or when
clocks ran slow and blood sped.
Then their eyes saw vistas and the ant
upon the grass. The sweep of lake
and mountains, love's vagaries,
the way a breeze stirred a flower—
these tethered the days;
the sun and moon on time's smiling face blessed
the breath that moved their limbs with grace.
Life stirred in coiled leaves, and the ant
teetering on a blade hurried toward a crumb,
as they, heedless, hurried on their way.

When spring touched with fire every living thing,
who would know the granary with its open door,
the scattered seeds, the names half-hidden, faded,
the stones in the fields blossoming with snow?

When lips are used to kissing, laughter,
who would know this lowering sky,
    this mute gray,
angels with their sealed lips?
These   *these*   *these*   the birds speak,
flying in their vees.
For answer only the snow, a drifting flake.

THE STORYTELLER

I have died in your long dying,
relived with you in each retelling
each memory spun out and savored.
Today you explain the Venus's-flytrap:
how it is found near Wilmington,
and you cup your hands, seeing
the plant's sticky heart,
the filaments that trigger
the leaves to close.
Nearly blind, nearly helpless,
once you pulled banners from a hat,
bouquets from a pocket,
made coins and cards disappear.
Even now your hands can be a plant
or reach out to pet a dog dead
for fifty years or point
like a gun the way you used to do,
holding a child spellbound.
"Ping," you said, and the bear fell dead.
"Zip," you said, and doves appeared.
Only your body is wheelchair bound.
"In India—it's the strangest thing—
monkeys and peacocks sense
when monsoons are coming.
Monkeys howl,
and peacocks scream.
Imagine that!," you say.

Silent, I am listening,
foreseeing that dark wind
that will not leave me standing,
the rushing rain
that will drown all memory,
even these words that thrum
like your valiant heart,
making from air a cruel
and wondrous world.

ON SUCH A DAY

for my father on his 89th birthday

Again pollen dusts the porch
with swirls of gold the wind has swept,
and chains of flowers, mint-pale,
wave from column and trellis;

jasmine stirs, and the tea olive
wafts a siren song to bees
already drunk on holly bloom.
The fecund earth swells like a foaling mare.

No wonder that on such a day when oak leaves
at last let go their shriveled holds
and blow in a warm, soft wind,
that our Lord brushed away grave clothes

as oak trees do.
But mounds of leaves pile up
the years that will not go away.
Smiling, bent, wheel-chair bound
but sitting on the porch, nearly blinded
with glaucoma and with the paper tilted
to catch the light, you put down the paper
to talk of the past, or I do.

You come up the walk and it is spring,
Knoxville, perhaps, or Memphis,
on your head a straw sailor hat;
you drop your sample case
to lift me up high,
and you smell of cigarettes,
automobiles, hotels.
Today the oak leaves
are pages of a calendar,
so many floating near the porch,
piling near the corners.

Last fall you wore a beret,
carried a silver-tipped cane,
Maurice Chevalier, valiant, blithe,
talking of travel.
After a winter of pneumonia,
you are cheerful yet.

This April day I observe
how new leaves hang in the oaks,
small, lacy, reminding me
of something barely born,
wet and helpless, wings unopened.
If I could wish on a leaf,
like on a star, perhaps

I would see you coming down the walk,
and I would run, be lifted high, high,
to touch the leaves, hanging
green and waiting like tomorrow.

A BOUQUET FOR LESLIE

I.
They held no significance,
taken for granted as love is;
though now it seems
they were everywhere
in your growing-up years—
roses in our ramshackle garden,
beautiful but untended;
roses sent by all the boys
who were in love with you—
bud vase, corsage.
Once there were roses
in the living room
and others in the den—sent by two.
We laughed then.

Now nineteen silk roses
—one for each year—
bloom on your piano.
Silk, piano, carved stone—
all inanimate things endure.
But love does too.
It cannot be killed
or torn from the stem.

The roses are you now—
the essence of all things lovely,
loved.
Yet the roses haunt and hurt and cloy
and comfort little.
I am entangled in their thorns
and sweetness.
And oh they are everywhere, everywhere.

II.
Above your grave a crocus in the snow,
flaming candle briefer than grass,
tiny mockery that says so much
and nothing at all
to one who stands empty-handed, empty-hearted,
above the crocus, looking down;
for I have found no philosophy in flowers
or in seasons, in words or cycles.
Dry-eyed, dry-hearted, I observe
as one removed and far away.
I only know—
above your grave a crocus in the snow.

III.
April returns with a Judas-kiss of flowers,
April, greener than I remember.
There are violets this year,
thin stems above heart-shaped leaves.
You never saw them,
nor the jasmine, the irises, all new,
planted since then.
People keep on planting
as if it made a difference,
plowing and building.
It is the habit of living,
like the routine of seasons
returning in spite of all death.
And so I welcome April
with something less than trust,
and wonder if you
forgive us these flowers,
you, who were all our spring.

WHAT THE WIND KNEW

The way the wind came back,
a note or two humming
in the window screens,
I almost thought it knew
and softened its voice,
but seasons do not know,
do not mourn for summers,
for springs,
for the death of any lovely thing.
Leaves fall, leaves come back again,
and we are left to wonder,
knowing seasons return,
cycles, summers, noons,
but not the same leaves,
not the same flowers,
not the same hours,
and never you.

AN EMPTY VASE

The roses weren't you.
They never were.
Seventeen years discolored
the white ones gray
until they were an old wound
aching in rain,
not pain, but a remembrance
of pain.

When I put them there,
each silk flower
was too perfect,
but I could count them
one by one:
nineteen roses on the piano
where hour by hour
you played, long slender fingers
stretching out
like tomorrows fading,
chords and notes
never to be heard,
scions ungrafted.

Today I took them
from the vase,
washed it and placed it
where it would catch the light.
I remember your hair
catching the light.
Nothing was more alive,
crackling silk
like silk roses.
Strange, but they are still there.
They will always be there
even though I know
they were never you.

WHAT THE ROSES SAY

Ashes in the wind, ashes in the wind,
the bending roses say:
blush upon the blossom,
wing upon the bird,
leaf that flies tomorrow,
ears that have heard
songs in grass and meadows,
songs of flying birds,
all the merry children dancing in a ring,
all the lovers lying where the willows lean,
all the swollen flowers heavy with perfume,
streams that sing beneath a gibbous moon.
Quiet as the flutter of a turning page,
roses speak: all, all are ashes in the wind,
the bending roses say
and, as if gathered into hands,
fling themselves away.

VOICE AMONG THE TREES

Spirits stir here and memory.
One rectangular room with two windows,
a door, a closet, and for years
it held her scent. It is still her room,
and I, an interloper even now.

In evening air the locusts' whine,
rising and dying, barely hides
the little voice among the trees,
the wispy screams, gone for twenty years,
again calling *Red Rover, Red Rover.*

Grass knows. Sometimes it holds
the print of small feet running.
Haven't you seen them, especially in dew?
And the swing? It isn't always the wind
that makes it move.

Often I catch a glimpse at the edge
of my eye, an awareness, a slight
shift of air, like the way auburn hair
once moved, shining and swaying.
Yes, there are ghosts. Many.

One has a husky laugh; one reads poetry.
They live here, moving curtains, walking
among flowers, whispering in moonlight.
As we sleep, they touch us, kiss us goodnight.
I wonder if I smile? I feel I do.

WHAT YOU WERE

Mother, I remember how for days,
months, half-crazy with loss,
I fingered the small things that belonged to you,
stubs, receipts, clothes, your writing
on a scrap of paper, your spectacles.
I held to dead inanimate things.

Now they are gone, most of them—
stubs, receipts scattered;
I wore your clothes, gave others away
as you would have wanted.
The writing has faded; ink, illegible.
The spectacles, contributed to a cause,
are in India now.
Perhaps some guru steps into the Ganges,
seeing clearly the river of life flowing.

I know now that what you were
is not in the grave, in bones, in grass or glass,
or on paper or even in my memory alone.
Shaped by you, I wear your print indelibly
as I wore your clothes,
cloth and flesh conformed.
In my mirrored eye
I catch a glimpse of both of us,
a small reflection.
I hear my laughter and I know
this earth will always wear your print,
a faint gleam of light,
an echo intangible as love.

VANISHING

for Mary Dishman

Each time I returned, there was less.
Things disappeared—
dishes, lamps, bedspreads, doilies—
until her apartment was Spartan as a cell.
"I am giving things away," she told me,
"now, while I can, while I am living.
Things I once thought important aren't."
Over the years, the rooms emptied
just as she faded, patchy with vitiligo,
pale and perfumed as the tangle of hair nets,
the powder that spread across the dresser.
White panels hung limp or moved in a draft
at the windows while she slept
in a chair before the rolling screen
of the television. In the kitchen
the faucet dripped to stave off freezing,
the way an IV forms its drops
to steady a faltering heart.
When the call came a winter later,
I knew the faucet dripped again
in a bare apartment, heard it in my mind,
how it slowed, then stopped.

AT AN AUCTION, MAYBE

The yellowed wedding portrait is cracked,
but the thin line was always there.
For they were separate and very young,
and so they smiled with bravado,
their eyes bright as two new rings.

Snapped hurriedly in front of dim houses,
candid shots in black and white
show children between them,
one holding her hand, one his.
The light is harsh, shadow-filled.
Their blurred faces stare strained into sunlight.
Behind them a car shines under the trees,
as quaintly dated as their clothes,
her bouffant skirts, his army uniform.

Better times and later cameras reveal
Christmases amid a splendor of wrappings,
trees all alike though in color now,
and there are usual tourists' sights,
silly costumes at parties.

But the last pages are almost blank
with little to show of how they aged,
of how when she looked at him she saw herself
or how when he held her hand he was holding
    his own.
This is the place for the perfect portrait,
the long history that had made them
one riftless flesh, one melded bone.

A WHIRLING IN THE STARS

On summer's shadowy porch
I read in failing light.
Dorothy Thompson and Sinclair Lewis,
with strained smiles, pose arm-in-arm,
he in felt fedora, she in cloche,
behind them cars rattling and honking.
He has received the Nobel prize.
She will interview Hitler.
The caption reads, "1930
in front of the Brandenburg Gate."
In that dim world
Mother wore her foxes,
Dad drove the flivver bouncing
down muddy New England roads,
both unaware that I would ever be.
Though no passing breeze
or drop of rain knew my name,
perhaps something stirred,
a whirling in the stars,
like a pointillist painting.
I wonder too that I am here to see
how behind the trees pink clouds appear,
caught on branches like ornaments.
Time too seems caught and held,
a memory of memories,
a twice-told tale.
In my hand, the book is a blur of light
where two smiling faces, both dead now,
squint toward me and toward
their dying sun.

FISHING FOR GOD

They are playing their little games
with this dying man
showing off their knowledge
like children. *The bedsores
will respond to better nutrition,*
thus a tube in the nose; *and keep him dry,*
thus a tube in the penis. Harpooned and
    helpless,
he tells me he wants to die and asks me to pray
that he will. I do. At 94 he has been through
enough, I know. I have loved and berated him,
the first man who had my heart, the one
who never had to earn it, the hero I knew
was never a hero, just part of me.
I pray to one I am beginning to doubt.
Be merciful strange, strange God,
who did not spare your son.
My father wants to die.
Love him as I do, as much.

And after a rest perhaps we may return,
bouncing down to the brickyard ponds,
the water quicksilver in sunlight,
my stride matching his, my hand clasping his
    thumb,
carrying home our catch, which we will offer
    you,
those shining bream, brief slivers of living,
rainbow scales, and brittle bones. Fragments
for you to feed a multitude. Until then,
we ask that you make an end of pain.
Give death.
And after, if anything at all, then, God,
you choose.

Still, I dream for him quiet pools,
summer air, a dog to hunt with, youth.
But whatever may be, grant this prayer
and cut him loose.

ON A KENTUCKY HILL

Walking as carefully as Geishas,
but with feet unbound, we nearly tiptoe.
I am in the center, carrying a red umbrella,
with sisters-in-law on either side.
Graves are all around, some collapsed,
many unmarked; this is shaky ground,
as tentative as an indrawn breath,

the wonder that life exists at all.
A light rain slicks pine needles,
softens the quaking earth.
In that corner where the fence posts meet,
their family lies; the father
drawn upward into pine,
a part of bark and needle, trodden
and resinous. Weeds sprout

among plastic flowers, stone slabs;
a can of dead roses rests on its side.
Some graves are marked only by rocks.
Little bones of nameless children bloom
in late asters or goldenrod, fingers of vines.
Here on a Kentucky hill I shrink down to size,
collapse inward, separate into grains of earth,
humus, wonder what, if anything, will abide,

knowing little will, that even the earth heaves
and falls, wrinkles with mountains,
takes the bones, the names. But there is peace,
a stillness unutterable, not even sad.
It moves quietly like a bird singing somewhere off
or a tendril of rain that the wind moves
north toward what once was home.

BROKEN TRUST

April has come again
like the Greeks,
bearing gifts and promises,
all those lies and offerings.

So many springs have gone;
still, frothy green cannot hide
winter leaves blackening
and the pale twist of Indian pipes,

death's angel in the shade
like a white skull
and the bluebottle fly
with rainbows on its wings.

Faithless, flaunting April,
why do I listen,
open the gate of my heart?
You are a painted corpse,

a wooden horse.
Wisteria droops
purple plumes
from every limb,

and dogwoods
stand ankle-deep in decay,
whispering, *Believe again,
but beware.*

THE LOST CHILDREN

for Ann Sanders

Calling it "having an adventure,"
we packed a lunch, set out early,
the periphery of town our uncharted world.
Rich Partin's corn waved above our heads
where we trudged, pretending to be lost.
Down in the bottom near Pickard's lot,
we shivered in the shadows,
caught in blackberry brambles and
    afraid of snakes.
Later, we set out for Syble's,
drawn by her barn, only a block from the square,
a swinging rope, bales of hay.
Lunch over, we climbed and jumped
until hunger at last drew us home.

Strangers asked where we had been;
even the police car slowed, followed us.
We looked at each other, stunned.
Then dimly in twilight I could make out
a crowd near the path. A switch nipped
    my knees.
Ruth swatted at you. We tried not to laugh,
amazed at the fuss, the hour, the lost afternoon.
That night in bed, I wondered how
those hours had fled, how the sun had moved
and neither of us had known.
My friend, time's sorcery,
other travels, lesser dreams
have not changed everything.

The dew on papery shucks,
the smell of wet brown tassels,
the prickly hay, laughter and
screams, warm Kool-Aid and cookies
in the shade, I taste them, feel them yet.
Tomorrow, let's pack a lunch,
cool champagne in a coal mine spring.
We'll talk all afternoon,
bury our goblets in sand,
then cork a note in our bottle
and watch it float down the stream,
past the shoals and snags,
borne on a ribbon of light.
Time will run slowly as molten gold.
And the note will say, *Gone*.

IV

What the Moon Knows

HAMBIDGE WOODS

Torrents pour over the rim, glass-thin,
then cascade and upcurl, reflect the flash and spill
of broken light, cool the rising moon.

A spiral sends up a milky plume,
a blossom of spray.
Trilliums are scattered on a trail

wet with mist, slick with pine.
White stars drift underfoot and overhead
appear one by one until the sky

is awash, foaming with trilliums.
I recall my father's eyes,
a flicker as a wick went out,

so small a thing, no more than stir
of wing or wind, an updraft
from the waterfall.

Now an owl repeats all night
the brevity of fame, and deep among ferns
foxfire makes darkness bloom.

WHISPERS

I.
The feeder under the eaves rocks, bounces
with wind, with the flutter of sparrows,
their squabbles as they fight and feed.
Leaf buds dark and small as thorns,
dogwood limbs whiplash, bend.
On the windowsill paperwhites unfurl,
permeate the room with a fragrance
innocent as soap.
Wind and wings and limbs,
forced flowers—
there are no other signs, no other sounds,
but…listen. A light rain begins.
Spring is breathing.

II.
Taste it now, this dying sun,
a wafer on your tongue;
drink the wine-sweet air.
Then count the beads of all your days,
press them between finger and thumb.
Whisper each one.

III.
The way water slides up the beach in a susurrus of
foam,
retreats,
and a crescent of sand sighs after,
the way
the moon summons a cloud,
the way a hand brushes
a shoulder in passing or a sunflower turns, listening
to light—
so autumn makes its long goodbye,
an *om* the wind bears
and carries aloft.

IV.
There are voices at night in the woods—
have you heard them?—
leaves muttering and birds
coming home.
Something speaks in the breeze,
the breath of a falling leaf on its way somewhere,
the stretch of growing things, spores and seeds,
ramblings of rain.
The creek boils over rocks
or in drought trickles into moss,
as if it were new, as if it had not worn
the stones smooth.
The dead speak all night long, repeat
what they can't let go.
Layer upon layer
like crumbling leaf-mold,
dry voices crackle in the wind,
sift and shift.
Hear the stirrings, the foragings—
the mouse on his timorous trail, a brown
barn-owl, a flap of wings—
while all night long, the dead talk,
remembering and living again.
Shhh, they say,
this is the way it happened.

GRASS

Something says *forever*,
a genetic memory perhaps,
the first time man broke seeds,
scattered them in his palm
and tasted them, wondering,
the first time he saw cattle,
sea waves of it stretching
to the horizon, herds grazing.
We know the juice of it but seek to extract
some sweet elixir, a *pastis*
smoky with green, piquant as leaves,
something more, secrets of the years
in bread and grain.

Yesterday I saw the way it flourished,
weed and clover-ridden, a farmhouse lawn
folding into mountains, evening
coming on with dampness, dew.
We wondered about fireflies:
had they all disappeared?
Just then they were there,
one by one rising
in the old way, yellow language
of mating, those lovers' lanterns
reflected in first stars.

Upon a farmhouse lawn
all was restored—
the fireflies, the child I was,
new, running, jumping,
a daughter matured, the husband
whose life was spared through surgery,

kept by providence like grain
that fed Hebrews, foretold in myth
and dreams. Some stillness
illumined the summer air,
a contemplation quiet as wings.

Blessed blessed, the wind said,
whispering through the bending blades.
Hear it now, the moan of it, the stirring.
Job returning from near-death,
his children back again,
and fireflies flicking above the grass.

ADAGIO FOR VOICE AND STRINGS

Last spring I put my hand upon a tree
and felt a breathing in the leaves
and saw in the rose's yellow eye
a corona like the sun's.
The earth stirred green and hummed.

In late summer a voice beckoned.
I am as certain of it as of dew
that sags from webs, heavy with light,
or sun that flames in the pond
and silvers the slow lap of water.
I heard it. It knew my name.

Now, in autumn and fainter
than the lace-thin moon,
fainter than the season's slow chords,
it is there, solo profundo, rich and deep,
summoning me once more

to hear the breath of leaves,
to love the roses, musky
and full-blown.

Before the fire, remembering,
shall I see their image on the pane,
and find in traceries of frost and flame
roses yet in bloom?
And shall I hear a voice in wind
when winter comes again…

when winter comes…

TO LOVE

> *...learn a little what it is to love. First, a leaf...*
> —Truman Capote, *The Grass Harp*

This tangible thing,
veined and hand-shaped, star-shaped,
helpless as flesh and as mysterious,
a life in contemplation
would not be enough
to understand your smallest structure,
and the way in autumn
you burn with inward fire, crumble,
the dust of you rising like smoke.
A leaf, a universe. I shall start with you.

From breath and from spirit,
made of air and fire,
the words of love and poetry rise
and fly like leaves carried by wind and weather,
whither? Toward black water,
layers of decay,
the moon's implacable solitude,
the future with its marble face.
All is question.
But for now...

I shall love a leaf, and then
a man, and then man, and then death
and what comes after. But first,
a leaf.

NO STOLEN FIRE

There are no eagles
to rend this aging flesh;
no grandeur of stolen fire,
only the petty plodding
of little sins; yet
his hell is parceled out.

My father's hands
twitch and fidget, his wrists
bruised with needles
where IVs infiltrate.
His feet will not be still;
breathless, he is dancing.

He is high and happy,
not on the bootleg hootch
of the twenties, but on steroids;
half-deaf, half-blind,
but sixteen tonight
and prattling of a man
named Meade who cheated him
seventy years ago.
"I found twenty," he explains,
"and lent him ten.
But he never paid it back."

He will get better. There is more
to suffer, weeks yet of regret
and old debts to recall,
a heart that holds a memory
for beaky birds to gnaw.
The monitors chirp,
counting his pulse.

Above the hospital
in twilight melee,
hundreds of chimney swifts
are fluttering,
random as the universe.

PATCHWORK

Over interstates and mountains,
through the tunnel Boone never knew,
we make our way to a Western Sizzlin'.
Mostly strangers, we embrace.
No one here closer than a cousin,
but one across the room has my mother's eyes.

I stare into a past distant as the moon
that rises above strip mines and trailers.
Groups swap tales; accents revive.
"When moonshine won't bead,
t'ain't fit for hogs," Pap said,
but tested it on his pigs.
"Hell, they laid around half-dead,
then squealed all day for water."

Stories grow funnier, sadder,
a miasma of mountain fog covering
what can't be told, the bleakness of lack.
"Next year," we say, and know
it has taken forty years to bring us here,
Appalachia's diaspora.

Next day, down roads twisting
into hollows cool as a dipper of water,
we convoy to what was their farm.

The old ones, the ones we never knew,
lie under that knoll. I breathe an air
so clean it seems it has never been breathed,
while jarflies harangue from every tree.

Gone to seed, grass weaves hymns,
lining out names: James and Annie,
Reed, Joshua who died young.
And I imagine the rhythm of looms, churns,
twang of Jews' harp, the click of needles.

We make our way back to the cars,
knowing we may never return,
our lives a patchwork of velvet and denim,
a crazy quilt of all they wrested of comfort,
a sturdy beauty, their children
and their most enduring art.

PERCEPTION

What is real doesn't matter, only what we perceive to be real.
—Author Unknown

Home is a place that never was,
where hills were mountains,
where no one grew old
or died, where love held your hand
before sleep came, those summer nights
when the moon was late, and insects shrilled.
When air grew damp, fog came
creeping into the valleys, winding
down narrow roads, like some cloud
of death, Aaron's curse, and morning
brought locusts rasping from every elm.
Pharaoh, Pharaoh, a rattle of wings
undulant and melancholy,
the season's elegy endlessly retold.

Home is a place where counters
were galvanized, where iceboxes soured,
where lead pipes poisoned,
but the water was sweet and tasted of mountain.
Every wall had a tale to tell;
and in the fireplace, zinnias ignited
—chartreuse, ochre, hot pink—
smoldering colors warm as summer.
All was cheap:
doilies, dime store dishes, cretonne on pillows,
but no one cared. Closets bulged with jars:
green beans, kraut, and the smokehouse
held bacon grainy with salt.

After supper the old ones watched the sun go down,
swatted flies and mosquitoes,
waiting for the rooms to cool.
It remains, that house, that porch,
caught in a time-warp where places go
that never were. I visit it often, hear the swing,
the screen door, voices calling my name.
Bike- and skate-tired, I run across a lawn
lost in shadows, calling,
Mother, Mother, I'm here. I'm home.

ORION

for my father

Beginning,
you hunted muskrats
your brother's knapsack on your shoulder,
Drive, that faithful dog, beside you.
Rambling to the river, to the woods,
adventuring and running away,
you took a ship to Europe, then sailed
like Twain, up the Mississippi, studied
the treachery of snags and currents, steering,
and later rode horseback into the hills,
selling whatever could be sold,
then around the world, down the Amazon,
outliving a dozen dogs, two wives,
a world that never grew old to you
though you did, though you wore
beyond wearing, frail and breathless,
nearly blind, nearly deaf,
until you took death
in your mouth like a pill
and swallowed it, traveling
to the lees and beyond, crossing
the North Sea, feeling for icebergs,
feeling death
like the cold wind off the ice, and
nothing above but stars.
Your sea-blue eyes still filled with love
for the kingdoms of this world,
you left it, setting out alone
like a boy hunting,
a knapsack on his back,
beginning.

INTERMISSION

At the Corner Drug,
a fluorescent moon glowed
above the fountain, another
lit the dark interior and on the door
a sign read, "Gone to the theater."
At Jack's we sipped cherry cokes,
puffed on Kools,
talked above the thump
of thirty pairs of saddle oxfords
doing a boogie in the Blue Room
to Glenn Miller's "In the Mood,"
pausing and picking up the beat,
shuffle stomp stomp shuffle.

Scooting from booths,
some gathered up change,
shouldered their way outside,
bound for the Mitchell Theater
where John Wayne made war.
The real one had ended.
Under the marquee, boys
who had never heard of Korea
leaned on hoods or fenders,
faces shiny as chrome.
The broken courthouse clock
wheezed toward a chime
that never came.

Tangled in a cloud, a hook of moon
scythed the top of Ball Hill,
and a voice distant as a night bird
drew itself out in a sigh,
"My mom's going to kill me.
I swear."

APRIL 12, 1945

Where the house stood,
trees have come back
one by one, maples, elms.
Sweet is the shade of memory.
Shades walk there now
when evening returns.
Hear the pat pat of a rocking chair,
see my grandfather's brogans
tapping the floor,
his hand cupped over the finial
at the top of his chair.
Far in the back Grandma rattles pans,
warming supper, heating the oven,
despite summer heat, the stifling kitchen.

The icebox door slams.
Over the sink a triangular mirror
just where it has always been,
blurred and chipped, cheap.
Cretonne on the sofa, the fireplace painted red,
a radio from a bedroom playing jazz. And Mother
adjusting her dress over slim hips;
plissé and chenille cover the beds.
I am wearing a playsuit, sandals,
and a satin bow, reading the comics
from a paper that says *Roosevelt Dead*.
Grandma calls, "Supper,"
while night beats against the screens,
and evening breathes,
sliding with fog over the mountain.

Light is tallow yellow, the color
of oil cloth on the table.
Wartime steak, pounded to a pulp,
is still tough to chew, though flavorful.
Gravy is rich as laughter; mother's biscuits
seem to float in air. We are all there:
Daddy Reed slightly drunk,
Aunt Effie mad at someone.
Grandma's head bent in prayer—
now all are gone, those bright hours.
I pour sorghum syrup, play with my fork, draw
in my mind a circle of light against the dark.

THIS EASTER, NASHVILLE

Out of the morning darkness
into the bus station, two men
and two women
with pale, worm-ridden children.
One woman is a slattern from the hills,
the other manicured and tawdry,
young, but with her teeth gone.
"Elaine," the tattooed man says
with a nasal twang, "buy me a cup of coffee.
Are you drankin'? You've got to quit
that drankin'. I ain't kiddin.'"

Steam from my cup
spirals up,
gray as the light
of the rising sun smearing
the windows,
and I think I have
lived this before and known
those children, wide-eyed, hungry.
And I cannot forget
the child I saw once
hit by a car and the way
she tried to stand up....

Over my cup silently
I pray: Forgive us,
protect us from fate, cruelty,
our own stupidities;
stay the hands that strike,
stop the tornado, the moving car,

keep safe those we love,
oh, love so foolishly,
knowing how bones break.

Bless the children in bus stations,
lank-haired, helpless,
the worn waitresses,
the tattooed hand holding
the last cigarette shaken
from a crumpled pack,
not because we deserve,
but because we humbly ask,
holding to the light
these hands of flesh and bone,
thin, breakable,
hands that can hold nails, like yours,
or a cup catching the light
of this day we are traveling,
have traveled, one day more
in all our unknowing.

ANCIENT FIRE: Kentucky's First House

Lifting and flapping, wild geese
shift in waves of honking flight
across the pond.
Harvesters that stair-step corn
to bin and barn are silent.
Autumn fog
and the chill of setting sun
settle with the paling sky,
a rind of moon.
In your palm you shift
arrowheads, then point
beyond the line of trees,
across the river to that third ridge.

"There," you say,
as if following the flight of geese.
On that knoll I know
they built the first cabin,
nursed their horses,
and planted peach trees
that would never thrive.

Gnarled apple and hickory
came to claim this place.
Wolf and deer belonged,
every hollow alive with game
stalked by Crow and Cherokee,
who paused to choose
flint and river rock,
shivering in the shade,
wary of a land that seemed
spirit-ridden,
haunted,
drenched in blood
and shadows.

Worn deep by moccasins
and boots, by hooves, paths
lie hidden now, thick with leaves
where bison traced their way to licks,
where trader and warrior,
frantic for heat, rubbed twigs.
Now autumn flames maple,
ignites with its slow embers
the lichened oaks,
and no one remembers
the fires that burned before
or that first house,
chimney of wattle and stone.

We stand still,
almost hear the sound
of a shifting log,
the hiss of sparks
borne toward the stars,
feel centuries coming on.

TESTAMENT

Try to forget, if you can, broken pines
left by loggers, burned-out brush,
how a double-wide erupts with children and dogs,
and how on a makeshift porch a sofa spills
its pale intestines. Try to forget the desolation
of blanched fields alive with grasshoppers,
how sagging shanties sprout hay, and the barn
leans, and no one comes except the postman,
and for miles the highway shimmers in a haze.
But you will remember loneliness,
how light reflects on the rim of an empty glass,
how a wasp sounds in the eaves. You will remember
the milky scent of new-born calves; the green moan
of fresh-cut meadow will never leave.
Memory is a dirt dauber's nest
with its small caves; it is the ache of sunset,
the drum of frogs down by the river,
despair that has no name.
There are things of value here. Sift through these.
Keep the touch of a gentle hand.
Recall how the moon came back just over the trees.
Remember peace. Remember rain.

CANTICLE IN SEPTEMBER

> *It is the lack of possibility that murders us.*
> —Kelly Cherry, Natural Theology

I.
His head is leonine, mouth soft, bred to retrieve.
Now he rolls on his back like a pup,
holds a ball between his paws,
then drops it into his mouth.

We are both old,
I in sunglasses,
his eyes ringed white with age.
Incongruous, I wear a Garfield shirt
and little else, barefooted.
But no one can see me
on my bench in a corner of the garden,
resting like my old dog in a spot of sun.

"Barney," I call, and his head
is under my hand.
"What plan gave us such natures?"
(He has his calling; I have mine.)
For reply, he drops the ball at my feet.

II.
A sweet scent breathed
from the holy water by the door.
It said *clean* like the nun's wimple
or forsythia opening on her desk.
The room smelled of chalkboard,
the starch of uniforms. All seemed innocent
though Sister Charles was short-tempered,
whipped everyone too much,

and the sacred heart of Jesus burned and bled.
I was pale, like some root-bound plant,
beyond tonic or Pluto water. Limp-haired,
prone to panic, not yet eleven,
I couldn't keep my socks up, and my feet hurt.

Jonquils bloomed down near the swings,
and the sky was blue as our chapel veils.
God saw everything, even the white spots
    in my nails
that counted my lies. I prayed for forgiveness
    and forgot,
sailing down the Mississippi with Jim and Huck.
From the refectory the smell of biscuits
mingled with the route of Magellan,
Sister's droning voice.
I bit my nails, decided
I would be a writer or a saint.
Outside the window, a path curled
into the garden, thick with winter leaves,
where Saint Francis, streaked with soot,
looked with pity at the budding world.

III.
Overhead, cicadas chirr off-key.
Gently, day-by-day, this change of weather,
this thickening of blood, thinning of bone,
everything letting go, a long, slow dying.
In the center of the birdbath, Saint Francis,
pensive, stares into the distance.
A redbird flirts, his song a rusty hinge.
Swarming, old words return,
the sound of someone beating erasers,
the hum of Gregorian chants.
Barney ambles away, and I remember
hands burning from a ruler,

forsythia, the refectory and the hill,
time stretching away like plowed fields.

IV.
A note of song,
high in the evening air,
rings like a vesper bell,
like a bird flung from a saint's hands
in some garden yet to be;
perhaps there I shall study
sainthood and poetry,
the ball of the world at my feet,
oh bright world ringed
with possibility.

REVISIONS

for William Stafford who said,
"You must revise your life."

If I could delete words,
add caresses, polish endlessly,
if I could rearrange the casting,
or form the clay to start again,
say all those things I never said,
add a softer hue, classical truth
or symmetry of line,
but I am left with this strange cup
that won't hold tears,
this doggerel that bumps along the page,
this smeared canvas, warped frame,
a drama with too many acts,
language that trips on its tongue,
a muse that's not a harlot
or snaggle-toothed,
just mundane.
And I am left with eyes that see
all too well the critic's pen,
and a heart that knows
what can't be taken back
or done again. I have made
a pattern knotted past change.
There are no cantos here;
this is no vase to last a thousand years.
This is a life without revisions,
a scrawl and a whimper
and the plea *forgive*.

BEACH FIRES

Newly divorced,
the philosopher revealed
he had been so eaten by despair
that on a Maine beach, with night rolling in,
he piled stacks of driftwood
that stretched into a curve along the shore.
Straight-backed, torch in hand,
proud as an Olympian, he ran,
bent down and ignited each one.
Purpose? None, he said.
But exhaustion left him
somehow vindicated, somehow clean,
as if each pyre was a small sun,
and he was the god that made them burn,
nothing more than this. It was something to do,
something to say if anyone were listening,
as if it mattered, as if anyone cared.
Beyond the susurrus of unseen waves
endless and unfeeling, smoke joined fog,
voiceless in rising spirals,
like censers of incense or unspoken prayer.
And all along the beach,
fires winked out one by one.

BALM

Cicadas mourn in rasping vibratos
from tree to tree, while leaf by leaf
the summer is interred in gold.

The apple on the limb will fall and
even suns go out. Autumn's
sharpest pang will pierce

someone else, and other lips
will sing and kiss and pout,
know the stain of love lived

past death and gone. This leaf
finely veined, laced with light,
will not come again

though others may. In shadows
seeds lie dormant for a while
to live or never live at all.

Sulphur butterflies spiral
in endless dance; bees delve deep,
drinking autumn wine.

Lethe.   Opiate.   Balm of desire
to forget our summer ended
in pain and fire.

CHRISTINA'S WORLD

Alone is a word that stalls on the tongue,
chokes the throat; it is beyond solitude,
for it offers no choices. It is a landscape
barren and bleak, gone brown
with the last of the hay,
winter soon to come. Here she sits,
crippled, hair disheveled, one hand
clawing upward toward the house
on top of the treeless hill.
There is no sound but the wind,
the whirr of grasshoppers.
Gray as the empty sky, the house
with its open door calls her in.
Ladders lean against the roof.
She knows each room, the barn,
the clothes line, the world
from her window.
All is clean, scoured with light.
In the night, boards creak,
clapboards ring with cold.
Day and night her bones ache
with a nameless desire.

CHEROKEE AUTUMN

Leaves let go.
One almost hears them
chanting,
as they lift in air,
turning end over end,
rocking downward.
If leaves could sing,

it would be with drums,
with rattles,
the shuffle and rhythm
of legend, repeating
the song of what they were,
the call of life to sky
and sad as all the stars,

the light that spills
amber as the blood
of all that ripens, dies.
Leaves are lost in sunset,
slipping with shadows
along a trail that wanders
toward dust and dusk.

Still, they fall,
become the plum-rich night,
dark as the paths of heaven,
deep and alive.
Lit only by the moon, leaves
are speaking, barely audible,
telling tales of spirits and waters.

With sound of wind and crying,
with no more than a breath,
leaves let go.

MEDITATION AT SUMMER'S END

The sheet metal of noon, relentless,
curled wood, lifted shingles;
later, rain ran under the lintel
and water pooled.
A vine as if ordered,
as if it knew where to find
some vulnerability, crawled
tendril by tendril
until it wrapped a rusty nail,
stretched toward light,
strata of plank and rafter.
One nail gave way and then another.

Gravity and time? Whatever it was, the barn,
riddled by ant and worm,
powdered the hand when touched.
Three thunderstorms, a drought,
one wind, and then like an old dog,
arthritic, leaning, the barn swayed,
stayed that way for days.
First the gate, then the loft,
then the stalls shifted, tipped inward,
seemed to take a shuddering breath.

We never heard it when it happened,
but found it—a gray haystack—unrecognizable.
An artist sought boards for frames; snakes moved in.
At last we burned it, kept the hand-forged nails,
made compost. What causation,
what complicity of sun or rain?
All we know is that the barn fell
and a pathway of ashes
wends its way through roses.
Moon-eyed, bereft, the mousing owl
would tell us if he knew.

TIDAL MARSH

This world is white and blue and green,
and the air so sweet it makes me dizzy,
clean as the egrets whiter than bone;
reed grass moves as if a spirit breathed upon it
this way then that, as the tide sweeps in
or leaves. Grass sways from blue horizon
to blue horizon, and when the moon
calls the waters to sea, oysters reveal
their secret beds, and shrimp float
away to come again. Sparrows vie
for what is left, then fly away.
A heron stands silent as a cat.
Now the sky is hot pink, rippled with gold,
layered with lavender haze.
Darkness settles with the sun
as the tide moves quietly on.

THE CEDAR

Solomon knew them well,
those ancient cedars,
their sweetness an incense
for Jehovah's mound.
But no builder has scored this tree
or marked it for beam or joist.
It has sheltered only rain-soaked cows
or birds too wet to fly.
Storm-blasted, it is part of no plan,
subject instead to caprice and wind.
Now four long limbs and a topped-out trunk
reach toward a sky, blue and benign.
If it lives, little will testify
to what has happened here.

Solitary and exposed,
in the middle of a field,
it invites whatever fire may fall,
as if it beckoned Armageddon,
called down apocalypse
or any stray storm
to rattle the gates of hell.
Shabby but unbent, having weathered
one more winter, one more spring,
it stands like an old man,
not that sweet Kent,
devoted and unbowed,
but Lear perhaps,
cloakless and cold,
wandering the moors.

SHEPHERDS AT MIDNIGHT REMEMBER

Excitement ran ahead
as we came from hut and village;
children stopped their games.
There was something different,
what we didn't know,
but he made us believe in more
than solid earth,
the dust that sifted through
our hands and poured,
made us believe in more
than heat and cold.

But since he has gone,
we feel the chill;
and on moonless nights
alone upon the hills,
we recall the things he said,
recall the way we followed him,
forgot hunger, thirst, the lowering sky.
He said he was a shepherd too.

Once, words washed over us,
reached down inside,
cleansing as rain, the kind that makes
wild flowers grow, white briar-blossoms
among the tombs where a wild man raved.
Sometimes walking, we pass the cliff
where swine rushed into the sea,
the boat where, they say,
he woke from sleep
and calmed the waves.

Sometimes in the middle of the night
when only stars warm the sheepfolds,
and our breath blooms as we pray,
we talk about him, think perhaps
he is here, just beyond
the light of our fire;
and as clear as a mountain stream
that sings over rocks,
we almost hear him speak and see
hands reaching down to pull
a bit of grain, a man to life again,
a child to her feet.
Then someone says, "Listen."
And someone says, "It is a lamb
that cannot sleep."

THE CREATED

From this rough clay
pounded upon the wheel,
from this body made of dirt, spinning
like a wind lifted in that turning,
he is making a porcelain,
fired in the kiln and glowing,
a vessel of intricate filigree
planned and wrought
before the world was made,
of bones the bone-white
light, translucent.
He is making a finer thing
than could have been
without this molding.
Through pain, through loss,
through gain, through prayer,
through need
when we have called to him—all these
are but the trim of gold,
the leafy patterns encircling the rim
of what is beyond imagining.
See what he is creating
from this rough clay,
made by his own hand,
for his own hand,
to grace the table of a king.
Slowly we are forming.

RUFFED GROUSE BENEATH THE PICTURE WINDOW

You who made these wings
and formed such whirls
and patterns,
perhaps you save in some drawer
the design of brush and pen,
the draft and erasures
that formed the hollow bones.
I choose to think,
as one who writes, you keep it all,

that nothing of what you made
is wasted. Perhaps the wind
that lifts the zippered harmonies
is just your breath, blowing
this bird to life again in some
other place. Perhaps you take
it there and hold it in your hand
then release it to fly, no longer
broken-winged, and then again

being abundant in all you do,
lavish in color, plan,
you may begin again
with no less laughter,
fashioning fingerprints
and fronds in joy,
fashioning another song,
hands all red with clay.

FROST STUDY

In a welter of patterns,
blackberry vines survive,
twisted in their dying.

Angel-winged,
the begonia burns
with a cold Pentecost,

each tongue serrated,
tipped by white flames.
Only long strands of grass

lean untouched, directionless.
Colors shade
into plum, lavender, cerulean—

all rimed with the faint aura of ice.
So quickly it came,
in a breath, in a twinkling,

and left this meadow
a nunnery, passions burned away,
blossoms unremembered,

as if there were no other worlds,
no other resurrection or sweet
anointing of bees and trumpet vines.

But at night, under the frozen moon,
a seed sloughs off one filament,
shrugs it away, warmed by the pull

of celestial fire, some rapture
of green intensities
yet to be divined.

WILD GEESE IN MOONLIGHT

Across the sky, we follow them
as instinct guides their way;
their raucous song holds all
that we once dreamed:

spindrift and sails,
a bow that cuts the waves,
places we've never known
far beyond these hills

where night mist settles
over graves and fields,
where duty leaves us rooted,
mired deep in toil.

Still, our spirits,
earthbound, upward yearn,
almost set loose,
almost set free.

Hear them as they call,
high above the trees,
wild geese at night,
moonlight on their wings.

THE FEATHER

Beside the fence, next to the waterfall,
here is the feather I found,
so small a thing, and then I thought of you,
your longing for things that shine,
shards of sun.

As long as there's a newborn colt
to frolic, following his mother,
and time to see him drink, tail aflicker,
legs asprawl, and when she steps away,
he kicks his heels at play
and chases some imaginary creature
until he's tired and finds the shade;

as long as there's a meadow
where wind moves grass in waves
or there are ponds to shimmer
or storms that moan through pines;

as long as bees meander
or streams find their way
to spill and sing;
as long as moonlight silvers
or sunlight gilds each separate leaf,
then the stab of joy will bring
a cleansing, swift as summer rain.

Keep now this feather,
for your pocket, for your heart;
place it beside the stone
of all those other songs.

THE CHILDREN OF SUMMER

We write to taste life twice.
—Anais Nin

White banks of clover
draw them like bees.
A welter of scratches
and skinned knees, children
know the bliss of running,
choosing sides, choosing friends,
making a chain of flowers,
patting out mud pies.

Dirt-smeared and sweaty,
they taste sour grass,
split maypops and hold
on their tongues the fleshy seeds,
pick passionflowers
that wind along the fence,
sip nectar from honeysuckle.

Making pacts, telling secrets,
they climb trees,
bombard their enemies
with pawpaws and chinaberries,
take prisoners, make treaties,
tumble and get up again,
cry and sing until the sun sets
and fireflies appear;

then heavy-limbed and sleepy,
children watch the moon,
a silver quarter they're too tired to spend;
instead, they tuck it away
like a coin tied in a handkerchief,
kept for ice cream.

ANOTHER ROOM

There has been enough
of dread, enough of death
and dust and pale eggs
of spiders hidden under chairs,
of frugality and winter want.
There has been enough
of sacrifice, the spare and scant,
thin snows that blow
in swirls along the path.

Now spring offers
its rain-clean air. Birds flit
from twig to twig, jittery
with berries and seeds,
with so much green.
Spirea whirls into a nebula
of white, and forsythia,
wind-whipped and bent,
cannot hold its weight of gold.
All is lavish, bountiful,
and brief.

Winter's musty grief
I shall put away
like woolens
for another season.
No one will hear
the hinges of my heart
or know how lightly I stepped
through the open door.

TIDAL

For my husband before his surgery

Froth-tipped, pale green and relentless,
thinning until the light shines through,
then lifting and breaking, in sunlight, moonlight,
they move   recede   move forward   recede.
Wave after wave repeats endlessly
    how something stays,
how something leaves, and how
all come back again—moon, tides,
wind, streaks of rain, those restless seas.

And where one begins
and one ends, where wave blends into wave,
who can say? They move, thin, tip forward,
spread, recede, return endlessly.
As waves are so are we,
for I cannot say where I begin, where you do,
where you end, where I begin or end.

 So entangled, so melded,
a whole, as one piece of music, one sun,
one moon, one sea, your smallest breath, your death
and dying breath mine, all you are is all of me.
This then: wave blending into wave,
silver, green, thundering,
thinning, pouring, breaking.
One. We.

LAST WINTER

Nothing lasts, she thought—all is sham—
the sheen upon the rose,
the shine upon the stone.
Roses die; stones dry
when taken from the brook.
Upon the tree the maple leaf is gold;
plucked, the gold is gone.
And the sumac leaf

so filled with autumn's blood
darkens to wine when fall has fled
and wind comes rattling stalks,
tells its love to the shaking vines.
But she opened the door.
"Tell me again," she said:
"Tell me our love will last."

And so he smiled and kissed her,
in his hand autumn's last rose,
and in his pocket a polished stone;
behind him a cold wind blew.
"I'll love you forever," he said.
"to the grave and even beyond."
Until winter comes, she thought,
and, as she held him, felt his bones.

AUTUMN SNOW

All day it has been snowing leaves,
slow as any cloud could spill; but these
are only ghosts of snow, stories
ghosts can tell of what went on before
another came upon the scene or how
one stayed or died or went away.
They know the tale the dying tell;
they tell the tales the living know.

Birds that stayed too long to go
listen to wind that's almost still
except for the sound of leaves like sighs.
Birds flit from ground to tree and down,
and then they rise to fly. Nothing sings.

And yet I think I hear along the path
your quick sure step,
the way you once came whistling home,
your happiness a thread of song.

I say your name.
For answer only wind,
a kiss upon my cheek,
your remembered touch
upon my hair, and all around
autumn snow.
Lightly as a leaf
I let you go…
All day it has been snowing leaves,
flakes of fire on glowing coals.

WHAT THE MOON KNOWS

I.
It was a warm winter,
and he shoved the umbrella into my hand.
Mother commiserated,
why make her carry that?
Where have they gone?
Bone meal for worms now,
beyond moons and umbrellas,
Oh, but they loved me then,
loved each other for those hours.
Behind the shadow of the earth
there where the moon hides,
do spirit eyes
look down at the daughter
who stood with them those years ago
a block from Broad Street in Richmond?
Above the White Castle, the flickering neon,
the moon was sliced and devoured,
disappearing, just as bitterness, divorce,
and time would divide us. Then death.
That night on our way to the movies,
we stopped to stare above streetlights,
above the glare of streets
still rain-slick from a shower.
How many moons
since then, battering years
that cycle in supernovas, comets,
looking down on faces looking up,
shadows of Stonehenge and the Paleolithic,
battlefields and monuments,
and just us,
the callous and the hurt,
on our way to see Bette Davis
leave for Chicago in *Beyond the Forest.*

II.
Eons ago it seems, I took you by the hand
and led you to a shallow dune;
being daring, I wanted you
while waves foamed and retreated,
beneath stars and the shadows
of moonlight among sea oats.

You were hesitant, maybe shy,
but no one was near.
Whitecaps pounded in. And I,
elemental as Eve, whispered in your ear.
Temptress for only a little while.

Now I have a folded flag
covered with stars, and friends
whose words are lost to me.
Instead, I see your smile,
see other stars, faint pinpoints of fire
beyond your wide shoulders.

Tonight the moon rides high.
a grinning skull. It says that death is all.
It lies. For I lie close to you, sand scuffed,
replete, my lips swollen with your kisses,
and all around us the sea-white foam
hisses and retreats. I shall believe what I wish.
There is a sea in Eden, silver at the full.

III.
What the moon knows
is silence and an ice-blue solitude;
only a wandering star may appear
or a meteor to scatter
dead fire of craters now turned to dust.
Vast is the darkness; eons vaster still.

After the reapers, the last harvest,
there is no one to touch my hair,

not even the moonlight,
old moon hovering above the trees,
wrapped in a shawl of mist,
not even the breeze that lightly lilts
and bends the last roses, leaves them
scattered on the ground.

In what is left of autumn. I shiver thrice:
once for love, once for death.
And again for the moon
that knows.

LATE SPRING: The Widow Speaks

Others have known the seasons turn around,
winters come when dogwood should foam
upon the hills or have known
cold settle down in fog that lasts past noon.
Others have heard a tapping like a cane

upon some solitary way when rime encrusts the trees
backlit by a sky so blue it jolts,
holding bits of frost that float and dazzle
with flecks of fire, a sky touched with titanium
as if painted by Vermeer to chill a room with light.

Others have known an ache that cannot be stated,
some stirring that is all there is of spring,
as if grief were a bulb that curls upon itself
and moves within the hardened earth,
called by a voice that summons it to leaf.

Though others have known such pain,
have survived to tell the tale,
what is that to one who knows
this is your first spring under snow.

PROCESSIONAL IN GRAY

> *On the banks of the river of Time the sad procession of*
> *human generations is marching slowly to the grave...*
> —Bertrand Russell

Barely dawn, and down
by the river they are shuffling,
leaving no footprints.

They move like the fog that winds
between trees and slips through inlets
touching moss and cypress stump.

They are whispering as they walk, talking
to each other, their voices weightless
as a communion wafer on the tongue.

Above their heads, a bird's bright song
and a limb silvered by sun, the river
a dazzle of light, a mirror of sky

broken and alive. Cascades
of laughter in small waves lapping,
our voices from afar call, "Remember!"

But the walkers do not hear.
Nothing we say will matter.
Nothing we do. Their eyes are set

toward the grave, toward the deep earth,
grains of stone. The billows of storm
and lung are still. Their trade is bone.

In gray shadows they are walking,
complete and whole,
done with remembering.

SILENCES

The heart has silences.
Sorrow's words are few,
and it appears
almost as if a hand
slipped over a face and erased
something that could not be stated,
only known,

for I have seen eyes go flat,
light that sparkled there
become heavier than summer air
with the weight of storm,
air grown thick and still,
when only dust spirals and settles,
rises again. Then as if from afar, wind. Listen
to trees, the wrack and whip of bending limbs.

Storms pass,
but something lingers, unspoken.
It is there in a tatter of cloud,
in a rain-washed sky, where
the silent moon blows a silver horn.
You may never hear it. But the moon knows.
Sorrow knows it, too.

STORM'S END

                        A cool wind bends

tasselled grass,

                                  scattering

               seeds against the stone.

The light of a single

                                      star

glints on granite that bears

          your name.

                    Only the moon

                              remembers

how you loved the rain.

MOSS ON THE NORTH SIDE

As quietly as snow in deep woods
when a laden branch lets go,
and layer upon layer shifts down
until at last a rising wind
lifts the sifted flakes;

as quietly as moonlight
tips with midnight blue
the frost-encrusted limbs
of fir and spruce,
so does love leave,

almost traceless, no more than
a small print filling with snow.
Were there deer? Did one step here?
And was there someone who called
my name, touched me as I dreamed?

Under snow, a green whorl moves,
the coming spring no heart lets go,
like a fawn that cries for its mother,
out of view, moss on the north side
where she feeds.

A TURN OF SEASONS

Something in the summer
foretells the fall: roses as they bend and bloom,
fog on mountain roads,
the mockingbird's haphazard nest,
a meadow's wind-blown chaff—all are epitaph.

When it comes, I've known it all along,
the dusty crickets' requiem,
the high-pitched thrum of locusts,
mourning doves. And far above,
a cortege of chimney swifts at dawn.

All attest that nothing lasts:
wreath-strewn winter, the wheeling stars,
sleet that blows across the pond.

A keening wind bends grass and weeds
over graves of pioneers. Still, spring returns,
with earth's green fire, litanies of rain,
and I cannot doubt
the curled fern's cloven tongue
or dogwoods scattered on the hills.

V

Bearing the Print

ALL THOSE MORNINGS

waking,
it was your voice
I heard first—
gentle, sleepy, kind.

Last night I dreamed
of a lake
without a ripple,
conifers pointed skyward,

waterward,
until it was hard to tell
which image was real,
sky or water, just still,

a world with no clear rim,
a blend of colors and silence.
I wouldn't want to live there,
but I do—

TRIPTYCH FOR AUTUMN

left panel

Blossoms at the full,
feverish for a change of seasons,
a change of lovers, Don Juans,
whispering in plush seductions,
have stolen their way
up the trellis to a rendezvous.

Autumn cannot beguile again
with scarlet light
and blandishments of roses.
Impervious to lushness,
I welcome, instead, a dormancy,
pleadings of winter wind and snow.

I crave the taste
of bitter wine and bitter herb,
apples frozen in the bin.
Whatever spring returns,
there is an end to love.

center panel

When evening streaks and slants,
sunset ignites the orchard,
suffuses with gold the fruit
fallen in the grass.
Moving in the wind,
an Adirondack swing
faces the lake; light fills the slats
where they, long-married, leaned
content, summers ago.
Now grapes swag and droop,
twine garlands of vines
for autumn's funeral pyre.

Waves lap upon the shore
reach   retreat   reach
like hands that cannot meet
across such emptiness,
this darkening fire.
And still the swing
creaks   moves   creaks.

right panel

There should be no good-byes,
promises of a season softened by roses,
apples mellowed on the ground,
air turned to wine.

Though wrapped in woodsmoke
and gold, burnished with bronze,
autumn is exterior
to the farewell inside.

WINTER APPLES

for Sam

I.
Remnants on the trees
and faded into gold, last fall's apples yield
a feast for birds. Snowcapped,
leathery, for enterprising deer
or sharp-eyed raccoon, they are a gleaning
of cider and seeds, wineskins of poetry.
Nothing seems wasted.
Compost of leaves and loves,
the earth is alive with survivors;
what can we not keep? Cedar scent
of trees decayed, musk of apples,
harvests gone?

Old letters, found at the back of a drawer,
send up a sachet redolent of roses,
stir memories of summers ago. "Our love
will never die." Brittle as leaves,
the pages break apart.

Outside the window,
a robin-red breast, plump with song,
clings to a bough, recycling spring,
spilling snow.

II.
Perhaps a sulphur butterfly will light
upon silk flowers in fall,
and finding his mistake, fly on.

Perhaps cold rain will sound,
though we will not know,
and rain and snow
will gather in the traces
of our names.
Silent worlds apart,
we will not care.

But if I could watch forsythia sway
and see the dogwood bloom,
hear a warm wind come knocking
lightly at my tomb, I believe spring
could wake me though nothing could.

COOL WATER

for my father

Feverish, he can barely swallow,
so I feed him, spoonful
after spoonful of ice-cold water,
wish everything could be different
and remember Richmond,
the apartment where we lived,
being fourteen, the yellow light of the radio,
the Sons of the Pioneers
singing "Cool Water," his favorite song.

That fall in the vacant lot next door,
a silver maple quivered, the light
like water on leaves, each one
twisting in the wind, flipping
back and forth like coins
tossed to see who wins. But no one did.
Their marriage ended; winter came.
We packed and left.

Nothing was restored
nor returned nor made better,
no more than leaves return
once fallen in leaden heaps
upon the hardened ground.
But now that he is old
and in this bleak room,
we are together.
Nurses appear and disappear.

I bring ice, wipe his forehead,
recall the cascading melody
that made him smile.
And spoon by spoon
I measure out years, wasted
beyond retrieval, yet found again,
like desert springs or trickling pools.

USED CLOTHES

an Easter elegy

Those patent-leather shoes,
I bumped the toes together
to make them thump
and wore them out of the store,
knowing a Sunday morning biscuit
would restore lost shine.
Why do I think of that?
Perhaps because it was easy
to renew what was worn or old.

Today on the curb I place
three sacks of clothes: sweaters,
shirts. Opening one,
I try to breathe you in.
There is nothing here
but must and mildew,
no old-man smell, no urine,
no cologne, all stored too long;
and yet, I see shoulders
beneath that sweater,
feel the bones.

The cocoon of clothing
we grew into, out of,
all the paraphernalia of living—
how much there is,
but of you, nothing
is left for me to touch,
just these threads and ravelings.
A half-smile, a gentle hand,
the rumbling of voice and breath
will be worn again, we are told,
toe-bumping new, biscuit-clean.

THE TRAVELER

Always loquacious, even in illness
my father chattered on.
That April, Hale-Bopp appeared,
a blurry mist just above the trees,
coldly mysterious, silent as God.
I watched and wondered, thought of Twain,
how Halley's hailed his birth and death.

My father, too, had sailed the Mississippi,
marked depths and sandbars as a youth.
At ninety-four, life to him was still adventure.
Animated, he relived each memory:
the Amazon, India's beggars,
Kilimanjaro, and places he hunted as a boy.

By May, silences grew vast, distances
too far to travel even for one who loved it all.
By June, quietly as it came, the comet moved on,
my father to worlds beyond the sun,
meeting Twain, perhaps, to share a tale,
to speak with Socrates.

DESCENDANT

Fully hafted, of the Woodland Period
(2000 BCE – 1000 AD)

In a Virginia cave
it lay perhaps a thousand years
buried in sand, until that day
my father held it in his hands.
Only fourteen, awestruck,
he was silent for once,
aware of history.

When he was nearly ninety,
I asked him to will it to me.
He said, "Things have a way
of getting away from us.
You better take it now."
We both clasped cold stone,
and time was no more than a long scroll
unwinding the years.
His arthritic hands, large-knuckled,
looked for all the world like a caveman's.
"I wonder how many hands have held this,"
I said, and felt the sting of tears,
thinking of the passing of a blessing….

Now he is gone, and I hold the ax,
see blue-veined, thin-skinned,
gentle hands, awkward, nervous hands,
fingers once stained by nicotine,
always moving as he told his tales.
Beyond his hands are others, greasy,
dark and scarred, and mine overlapping.

I hear the long howl of wolves,
hungry beneath the shadows of trees,
see their matted coats in dim light,
and imagine the security of stone,
how it could fend off whatever moved.

Carved in little triangles,
ticks that measured time
decorate the dark surface,
time that passed until it wore the ax
to half its length.
Outliving the dust of men,
bison, wolves, and wolverine, it rests now
as I lift it to the light and ponder
past and future, all those hands,
all we keep, all we pass on.

VOICES

The roundness of a river stone
forms upon the river foam
a small oh,
and that is all it speaks.

Above the marsh
one low cloud
follows a tidal path
and makes no sound.

A curling leaf loops down,
touches the ground
and settles with a whisper
so quiet only grass can hear.

On winter shafts of air
when wind lifts fallen snow
to rise again, we cannot know
what seeds are speaking

what prayers.

PORTENT

The dragon
is lashing his tail.
His fiery breath has left the red
in sumac leaf,
bronze that burns in oak and elm,
smoke that settles in the fields
before the sun. And now
his tongue licks the hills,
flicks along the fence,
and splits the tops of trees.
In the dragon's wake,
there arises such a keening
as wind makes
or women who weep
for those laid underground.
Leaves are flung like falcons
toward the clouds.
The battle will be lost.
The flag of summer fails.

BEARING THE PRINT

I.
Autumn mist swirls above the river,
the souls of the dead they say.

Water birds ask muffled questions.
Sound is a slow drum
that becomes the rain.

In my hand I hold a fern fossil,
each leaf almost alive,
like memory, but never green again.

II.
My hand upon your back,
your neck, a bump on your shoulder,
how well my hands knew you,
even now I feel the touch of silk,
feel the slide, the curve and dents,
the small of your back,
the rise and fall of love.
All is kept: pressed flowers,
bearing the print of meadows,
springs ago,
tender as touch and as frail.

III.
Touch is all we know
of the gold *Logos*

of autumn's
most abstract lie:

the script of a leaf
in stone.

IV.
I stand here, bemused, numb,
while around me leaves fall,
curl around trees in mounds,
and the wind speaks
over and over again
accept   accept   accept.
Not even the leaves
can teach me how.

AUGUST MORNING

The dark pond ripples with light.
Sunflowers, listening, turn.
The *om* of morning sun slants
across the fields. Wet grass ignites.
The orchard is brimming with fire

as if night had never been,
except for a shofar moon
left behind with its pale song,
blowing the faithful to wake and live,
dead bones to rise.

TEST

Perhaps I can stand to listen
to certain music, remembering
how we loved it together,
remembering how we loved.
Perhaps I can stand to see
blue mountains, streams,
go back to the inns we shared,
think of your happy face,
the way your body felt beside me
as we rested, quiet, the sound
of your gentle heartbeat.
Perhaps I can return to all
we knew then, the plans,
your face above a dish I served
and how you enjoyed
simple fare, lemon pie, bread. It is true
I may be able to do these things.
People do. So why not I?
I may be able to stand.

OLD SINS

In tattered shrouds, they return.
Grass moves where they move,
and as they pass, Spanish moss sways.

You can't outlive us, they say.
We never die. And from the cavern
of memory they rise with false faces
and painted smiles. Once I knew them well,
held their hands, for they were friends.

Now, old sins glide down empty halls,
smell of decay. Where little is left—a chair,
a candle stub—they drift, elemental as pain,
to touch the rockers on the porch
or move the swing with its rusty chains.

When fall chills the heart with rain,
they stay, settling like dust, faded, gray,
until spring mists the hills with green,
and pear trees spread white veils.

No one sees them go;
the wrought-iron gate swings closed.
Doves call, voices like waterfalls.

SOLILOQUY OF THE ROSE

Subtle as the Orient,
touched with musk
and midnight gardens,
my fragrance lingers
in evening air,
leaving a wisp of memory
as women do
who walk through spellbound rooms
and trail behind them when they go
a delicate perfume
that lingers like the afterglow
of day, a wake of light
before the moon appears.

And if there is no one here,
no one to care
when lovely women pass
as roses do,
then who shall grieve?
Perhaps some wandering bee may sense
an absence in the grass, some shift
or difference in the wind,
but sorrow does not exist for me.
I cannot weep for love or loss.

Though time strips away
roses, seasons, all loveliest things,
these for me are naught;
for beauty knows no seasons, is unaware
of moons that come or go.
Enough, to sway in summer storm.
Enough, to hold the trembling rain.
Joy is all I own.

WITHOUT SHELTER

Magnolia leaves lie black
upon the grass. Summer drought
tints air to an amber haze.
Little moves, except for a scattering
of branches clacking in a whirlpool of heat.
Chickens hunker down,
toss dust, or, lethargic, search for grain.
Corn stalks rustle, burned brown,
gone to fodder before the ears have formed.
Dread is a word unspoken, heavy as dark clouds
forming, a hard dry breeze
that intones, "You are doomed; you are doomed."

Behind the curtains, we search the horizon,
drop our voices like people at a funeral,
as if all things portentous require such whispers,
as if it mattered. In mid-beat,
Aunt May drops her spoon,
stares sightless, wild and frazzled.
And then it comes: rain, flat, horizontal.
The barn door crashes, sails past the tractor,
hurls over the fence. We dash for the hall,
but Grandmother rocks in her chair, refuses to move.

Mouths dry, we beg to be spared,
just this once, just once more. Knowing
how capricious the god of wind and rain,
we drop to our knees.
Each in his own heart pleads, each alone.
High noon, and yet there is the four o'clock train.
And then again, there is no sound
except the exhaling of air, and someone says,
"Lord, we must move from here. I saw
the transformer go. It looked like lightning."
We wait, listen, for what we fear.

Sirens.   Screams.   Grandmother sobs,
"Thank you, God. Help all in pain."
Stunned, we look at our hands,
fingers, toes, feet; we cling briefly,
then run out, blinded by rain,
a stream of blood washing our eyes,
observe the cow hanging in the cedar tree,
and slowly it comes to us: the meaning
of mercy, the meaning of grace,
and a plan we will never understand,
an imperfect world with a worm at its core.

WINTER'S TALE

Older than any story,
passion or revenge,
pages all unbound,
this first snow now
tells its wordless tale,
for there is no wind. Instead,
lightly as a pall,
death falls relentless and pure.
All seems inevitable,
at rest, until you feel
there may be something else
beyond the stillness,
no more than a hiss
as small flakes touch,
cling as they float past like ghosts.

Leaves, caught unaware,
have not fallen, and sag
to form shadows and cloisters,
canopies where faces hide,
demented and old. There is one.
There another. One wonders
where spirits wait and winter;
where they keep themselves
with their regrets, their burdens
of lost desire,
plans to hurt or hate again…

until some frozen night
when the moon is full,
and they can go about the earth
wandering to and fro.
Quickly, quickly now. Go.
Take with you nothing
but the pounding of your blood,
breath aching in your lungs.

Don't look back. It is enough
to feel upon your neck tremors of snow
and to hear the rising leaves
now whipping in the wind,
talking in tongues.

REVELATION

No apocalypse, seven deadly vials
poured out upon the cursed earth,
no locust with sting of fire
can bring a demise more painful than this,
no slamming of the tomb's iron door
can ring as loud
and leave forever a dark hall that will not end
except in ice and isolation,
no, none, not one of all those plagues
devised to torment man
can do what words can do,
spilled words that writhe like worms
in bilious venom and say,
"I tell you this because
you are my friend."

FORGIVENESS

Words ricochet from canyon wall to canyon wall,
grow louder over time. We say "I forgive,"
"I understand," and believe we can
until we hear the echoing of bullets
dead-on. In that prayer we say:
forgive us as we forgive, and try
yet can't let go. Petty, lacking nobility,
we revel instead in pain, and grieve
for the time before the words were said.
Unplanned, those cruelties are the worst,
blunt, truthful. Or truthful enough.
Eventually, it will come, cleansing
like desert rain, sending lizards hurrying
from under rocks where they have lain.

LOVE OUT OF TIME, OUT OF SEASON

When poetry won't come
and words lie heavy
like the pain of an old wound
that aches again,
or there seems reason
not to say what can't be said,
or reticence puts its finger on the lips,
think of this, my friend:
remember the fountain,
how water splashed and played,

made thin cascades of sound,
and all around, moon-lamps
made larger moons
than the small one
hooked above upon a cloud
in a campus sky, cerulean, rain-clean.
A poem waited in the broken branch
of a pear tree, a scepter of blossoms,
wet and frothy with spring.

But what was there to say?
Life determines what limb will break
and who shall love
or never will,
the vagaries of time and place,
seasons out of season,
the places we visit but never belong—

all this perhaps or just some little wisp of song
like a whistle in the night
when someone walks down a dark street,
hands in his pockets,
and sees pear trees in rain.
Write that one. Write it for me.

SIGNATURE: The Deep South

Jonquils have left their spears behind,
taken parchment blossoms;
saucer magnolias have disappeared,
violets, azaleas. Spring's surrender
lacks signature
though full-blown summer
states its terms in burning sun,
faded skies. May doubts,
qualifies with *perhaps*.
Juicy green remains,
the blaze of geraniums,
trees full-leaved,
the trumpet vine's reveille
in the fire burst of dawn.
Daylilies breathe their short lives,
and gardenias and jasmine,
those perfumed spies,
lure drunken bees
toward a ravishment of roses
who do not care,
shedding upon the grass
their scarlet dresses,
their bridal white.
With open arms
May foregoes might,
becomes "I will. I will."
Summer's treaty is signed.

FEAST

I am thankful for words
that taste sweet as plums
still cold from an icebox.
I am thankful, too, for a mad Welshman
reeling drunken home, spouting syllables,
and whom time held green and dying
while he sang.
Oh, for these and for others,
heads tilted back, eyes absorbing
moon and moth and yellow light,

for tales told on winter nights
and flavorful as apples before a fire
of one who killed an albatross
and changed at the sight
of sea-serpents writhing,
of a highwayman riding
into a dim inn-yard
while overhead a galleon tossed
in cloud-gray seas.

For calligraphy of bamboo leaves,
for the sparsity of words
shining like small carrots on white plates,
yet filling us feast-full
with all they need to say,
I am grateful.

For the gleam of waves on pebbles
that roar and crush in rising tides,
for sleeve-worn casements
and lights above the sea,

for dark blackberries of words
exploding with juice and sound,
for these, for all of these,
this is just to say...

they are delicious.

FOR WILLIAM MATTHEWS

Dead these nine years,
you who danced with me
in the barn at Bread Loaf.
I see your picture and remember
your poems, funny in the way
only the desperately sad
can write. In a wicker chair
you tore open envelopes,
smiled at fame that poured
like mail into your lap.

I remember how we all sang
"Hello, Mother, Hello Father,"
that last evening,
and the sweet Vermont breeze
lifting the sheer curtains.
If I could, I would bring it back
to you, that August night,
an awkward dance I had won
when you, kind gentleman,
held a stranger, guiding her
around the floor.

I would bring *you* back,
breathe into your mouth
the cleanest air
and poem after poem,
to set your heart racing,
to make you laugh again—
all of this I would do
for one who died too young

and would not remember me.

FLASH OF GREEN

So briefly
that quick green
just at that second
when the sun disappears,
and then nothing
except the way
the surf sounds,
and the clouds glow,
sun-caught.

So this brief fire,
pulse and breath,
shall leave behind
no sound, no tinge
of sea or cloud,
little at all of beauty
or remembrance,
less than a sky
lingering with flame;

yet we are told,
though faith's faint edge
may slip away,
there is within us
a kind of splendor
we fail to see,
a green, gold purity
that will rise beyond the rim
of dying day.

THE ART OF WINNING

When she could not accept
gratuitous evil or the status quo,
he would say,
"Hon, that's life,"
and touch her arm,
anchoring her to earth.

She has not changed
but has learned to walk around
the irremovable, soil
ground in, worn carpet
stained by living, her own face
in the mirror.

She stares some mornings
at a spot of sunlight
on his chair,
drinks coffee,
thinks about the way
light once touched his hair.

Evenings when the widows gather,
play cards, birds abandon
the feeder, nest and chuckle
as if they are watching
through the windows
the four of them chattering.

Then suddenly in the middle of a hand,
she recalls the way he was,
all that gentleness,
sees him whole,
the emptiness she owns,
all she holds of what is left,
discards what can't be kept,

calls, "I'm out,"
tallies the years
and just for now,
lets them go.

GRACE NOTES

embellish our days,
little echoes
that strike upon the heart
in tones simple
and complete....

In the western sky
a star, always there,
unnoticed till now.

Always, too, autumn,
the gold that comes
undeserved, bounty
of harvests, swollen
and bent with grain,
wheat shafts and seeds
feathered by wind,
soft, changing light,
the rustle of wings.
Fall spills its music
in chords, crimson
berries of sound.

When you came,
I knew what richness was,
melodies unheard till then,
harmonies unrehearsed, pure,
as in the evening sky
the whisper of a vesper star.
I think of you,
and chaos ripples into place.

COPPER HARBOR

The lighthouse casts no shadow
outlined against a sky where clouds,
snow-filled, glow from within,
like a canvas primed in pewter.
Its roof is a slash of red, incongruous
in so much lead, so much starkness.
The snow seems lithographed.
There is no sound except the fat slap
of waves against the stones the litter
of agates and granite ground smooth
by water. Only the windows
flash sliver, holding in each square
what is left of day, the bright alloy
of dying sun.

This is the way I felt when you left me,
everything falling into darkness,
a landscape painted
just before the light is gone.

FIRST SONG

Blue solitude of trees and a frozen lake,
so pure and expressionless, it is a face,
aloof and beyond touching
or a voice whispering.
Boughs drop burdens of snow
level-upon-level down.
Frost whirls and lifts, falls again.

Whatever tomorrow brings, a low cloud
portends a ragged curse on the wind.
But now a redbird begins his rusty song,
snaps small branches, and a deer
skitters on ice, stretches toward a low limb.
Sun clears the line of dark trees
with a dazzle of rainbows and white fire.

Listen. Below the ice, something sings.
Something sings.

WHEN BIRDS RETURN

Where is the man who fed the birds—
redpoll finches, chickadees?
Robins are here, the mockingbird;
they come but rarely linger.
The white doves are gone, rain crows, too.
If birds could, they might wonder,
or feel at least an absence.
Those full feeders that swayed in the wind
have been put away these years.
There is still the birdbath, left to rain,
and nests hidden in their old places,
wild berries, grass seed—scant fare
when once there was plenty.
When bird song comes again,
those brief and joyous notes,
somehow I always think
the birds remember.

DISAPPEARANCES

Where is the grandmother, thin and smiling,
she of the wiry strength with her voile dresses
and old lady comforts; where are the summer evenings
she sat with me on the porch and shared coffee
or patted my hand and called me Sue Ann;
where is she?
Where is the grandfather with his belly laugh,
the plump toothless man, who rubbed his bald head
and looked out at the mountains, thinking thoughts
he never shared;
where is he?

Where is the mother who fretted so much,
typing endless letters and tearing them up,
the mother who cooked pies and cakes
and biscuits that nearly floated,
the tortured mother who loved everyone
but herself; where is she?
And the daughter, lovely Leslie,
only nineteen when she left,
perfect and beautiful, with those deep dimples,
bending over me with her long shining hair,
and giving me that last kiss, "But I kissed you once!"
where is she?

And the father who wheezed out his stories,
tales of places he had been, detail after detail
recounted endlessly, the father who talked
but rarely listened, and could not hear if he had,
the man I loved so dearly, where is he?
And where is the husband who cherished me,
broad-shouldered, strong, calm,
oh sweet earth where still waters ran deep,
the very heart of me, where is he?

And where is the girl, the mother, the woman?
You see her shadow before you now.
Where is the one she used to be? Perhaps in a mist
that rises over a field or in a stream
that runs through mountains,
deep in grass, sun-warmed where she tumbles
like a child and laughs as she falls.
She is not here, that long lost child;
like the past and all that went before,
she has disappeared; she is gone.

THAT OCTOBER NIGHT

I never knew you well.
But today your obituary,
my high school classmate,
my age.
I can remember
a Halloween party,
a kissing contest,

dry lips hard-pressed
to dry lips,
and breathing
through noses.
I even remember
what I wore,
and how I hated Carla

bobbing for apples
and dressed like a princess.
I bobbed her head
under the water. I should have.
It was at Mack's house,
my first real crush.
And then this. You gone.

Mack gone. And I am living
Halloween, ragged, half-drowned,
surrounded by the grotesque—
never a princess, often a clown,
memory as clear as water
and bright as apples
that October night we won.

SOUNDLESS

He sits by her grave every day,
weather permitting,
sometimes in a chair he carries
or upon the ground.
He explains, "I feel closer
to her here."
I imagine what he cherishes,
what is left six feet under:
dust and bones and hair
or worse, some Hollywood
monster dried and purple.

He knows but doesn't care.
This is where he wants to be.
And so I walk away.
Nothing can be found
in sad notes rising to heaven,
the mourning dove's call,
nor in notes left on a stone
edged by grass
sending up fingers
toward the spring sun.

In dirge or celebration,
nothing is lessened
or magnified or preserved.
It just goes on endlessly
in some other form
somewhat like sound
in that forest where no one hears
or birds call or tears fall
no matter what we will.

IF I WERE A POET

I would wake each morning and hear
mountain streams rushing
through meadows where grass sings
with wind, warm with sun,
touched with shadows of wings
and clouds.

If I were a poet,
I would wake to your arms
around me, the gentle touch
of your hand upon my shoulder
and remember what it is to love.
My heart would stretch to meet
you with joy.

And at night from my window
I would see a hunter's moon
just over the horizon,
plump as a golden apple,
ripe with words waiting
for me to say. And I would say them

if I were a poet.

EACH YEAR AND ALWAYS

In a frenzy of feathered stripes
mockingbirds are mating,
fanning the air
with amorous play,
whirling lightly as dragonflies
above the lush grass.
I wonder, do they mate for life?
They do not care,
resting briefly now
on a green limb to begin again,
rising and falling
in a flutter of passion.
Soon their nest will hold
the responsibility of love,
and they will be
burdened with gathering,
all those hungry mouths
gaping and demanding.
But summer days can wait.
For there is only spring,
April's old song
amid a tangle of wings.

THE HISTORY OF A YELLOW LEAF

The history of a yellow leaf
is part of me. There are things
we do not need to learn:
the lineage of a maple tree,
the serpent's pedigree.

The genealogy of grief
requires no heraldry.
We sense a doom
when streaks at dawn forecast
impending storm, know in the bone
the red of alarm.

Some things cannot be taught—
the faithless lover's kiss that lingers long,
a honey on the tongue when winter comes.
In stinging memory, we taste the summer
when bees are gone.

MERLIN ON POETRY

Morgan le Fay collects words,
those she loves,
keeps them in a box
like so much dragon-gold
until they become her own.
She creates impressive spells.
But, Arthur, to go beyond
the joy of incantation,
to make *magic*, well...
See that green-scummed pond?
That's my trove.
It holds no gleaming pebble
like *solitude* or *cold rain*.
I do not shake it up
and bring out a bauble
to roll on my tongue
like dried fruit needing only
the juice of me to make it whole.
No one, not even I,
can plunge into that abyss at will.
It requires a summons.
A phrase or memory perhaps
will swim up, look at me
like some old turtle
missing a foot,
God knows how,
and our eyes lock;
the water rolls over me.
In those depths I peer up,
see my own face
staring down.
Then, Arthur, *then. You will know it.*
It lasts only a moment.
After it is gone, you swim.

BEYOND SURVIVAL

for Vera

I remember that other one,
a summer saved in watermelon rind,
but this, my friend, is different,
redolent of a frugal world
where pioneers burned barns for nails
before they plowed their way
into a deeper wilderness,
how they saved cracklings for bread,
made souse and scrapple,
patched together
patterns of fields and house,
fine stitches to warm
the hearth and years—all this
in the jar you gave. You explained
the yellow, the ripeness,
cucumbers gone past eating, but thrift
and brine and labor
save even these. I taste them now,
think of fall,
how all that is good is salvaged,
how nothing is wasted. My mouth
is alive with cloves and sweetness,
want is barred from the door,
and all of summer's bounty
blazes into gold.

WHAT DREAMS MAY COME

Struggling,
we rise like swimmers,
leaving the caverns,
the smoke-swirled
grottoes where fear thrashes
and breathes out dragon fire.

These are the dreams
we are afraid to recall,
water dreams where one sees
moving shadows as on a wall,

foretelling a future so dank
and chilled we are left like children
crying out for a mother
who no longer lives.

Then treading water,
we awake again, come
into the world we know
of familiar rooms, charted seas,

the maps and memories
time has made
into a painting by Monet,
lilies opening in lilacs and blues,
a pond on fire with sun.

A WINTER TEA

> *When you face your monsters, they will become*
> *your friends, even take tea with you.*
> —Mitch Peterson

Those blowzy frumps
have come uninvited,
plop down as if they belong.
"I'll have a drop
of pity," says Insecurity.
"No one ever loved you,"
says Resentment. "Now, now,"
Guilt intervenes. "Bruises and welts
would help my feelings,
a little flagellation,
but barring these,
I'll have a lump of sugar, please."
Resentment sips, then asks for lemon,
looks around and frowns.

"All for show, of course;
the silver is plated,
and these cookies are store-bought. Cheap."
"Delicious tea," Insecurity says,
trying to please.
"Oh, much too good for me,"
Guilt interjects;
and Resentment points out,
"Well, it will do, but it isn't Earl Grey."
All try to read the future
in leaves that won't be still.

The teapot is empty, cold.
They have taken out their knitting.
The clock on the mantle
ticks in the gloom. The coal in the grate
shifts to ash as a spider weaves a web
from table to chair, and a mouse retreats
with a scrap of cake.
Waking, Insecurity shudders
and gasps for air.
"Hush," says Resentment,
while Guilt dreams of a past
she can change.
At last their hostess sighs,
turns out the light,
and leaves them there.

WHITE MARBLE

> *Thousands of American servicemen were buried in Britain,
> their graves marked with white marble memorials.*
> —Realm, The Magazine of Britain's History and Countryside

How many remember
men who once smoked
their Luckies, drank their beer,
and dreamed of home.
Who remembers the bravado,
the swagger of uniforms,
the grins, the scent of gin
and damp woolen khaki,
handsome men flirting with girls
and thinking of stolen kisses.

Under the yew trees,
under the moon and the spires
where the owl calls their names
in shaded churchyards,
alone with white marble,
young men now less
than bones and dust
lie in rows as symmetrical
as platoons on parade.

Buses whiz by, and tourists
write postcards, in love with a land
damp and green with spring
where hedgerows wind out of sight,
tourists on their way to a lodging
where they will have tea and cakes
where they will sleep only a night.

ONCE MORE THIS FIRE

Autumn with its ache again,
its burden of watery light,
branches nearly bare.
Fleeting as bonfires,
frost has burned its etchings
in bronze and blood, rimed
with a tarnished line,
maple and alder, beech and elm.
Smoke carries away the incense
of wood chips and ashes,
scent of windfall pears.

Squalls of rain bring down
a rattle of acorns;
rain slants and streaks
across the ragged garden,
sweeps away as quickly
as it came. In evening's haze
sunset haunts a landscape
where ponds reflect remnants,
embers of sumac and poplar,
that lap and scatter
against quiet shores.

Slowly one red leaf,
caught in an updraft,
drifts.
Autumn
looking back
one more time.

OVERNIGHT THE WORLD HAD CHANGED

Always once in winter
that morning of the first snow,
when we as children pressed our noses
upon the pane, our exhaled breath
left lace. We traced it with our fingers,
made maps and circles. Beyond,
deer tracks wandered
a landscape clean
as an uncharted sea.

Journeys ago…
startled by love, breath indrawn,
I saw again a different view,
reserves of tenderness
and paths no one had known.
Overnight the world had changed.
A hand touched mine,
wound finger by finger
around my wrist in traceries,
familiar and strange.

Always once in spring
an open window brings
the scent of mint and rue;
light rain sweeps the sill.
A quicker breathing tells me, too,
that even love can come again.

VI

To Stitch a Summer Sky

WHAT STAYS WITH US

A tattoo snaking up her neck,
she sits on the trailer step,
touches her new teeth with her tongue
and looks out across
a rusted-out car,
a gutted washing machine,
to where the mountains

purple and fade in sunset.
By her feet, snow dusts a buttercup.
Life's not all flowers and sunsets,
she thinks, and laughs to herself.
Did a poet say that?
Cliché, she thinks, all is cliché,
certain bookish words forever hers.

She has a future; the woman
who handed her the GED
told her that, and she couldn't be wrong.
Shivering, she pulls her jacket tighter,
draws on her Marlboro.
With one glance backward,
she goes inside to cook soup beans
and watch the Jerry Springer show.

IN NORTH GEORGIA NEAR WARWOMAN DELL

Autumn lengthens toward dark,
a citron light that falls
mottled-plum,
pale persimmon, sienna tint
of whatever ripens, dies.
Voices murmur
in faint rustlings,
whispers that descend
in windless air, moon-still,
muffled by moss,
the rush of streams over stones.

Ridges away, in Cherokee,
high-stake bingo games thrum,
slot machines wheel, spill;
a man, deep-throated, calls out
"Under the 0, forty-two,"
and someone else yells,
"Aiiiii damn! BINGO!"
While on the outskirts,
black bears ravage tourists' cars,
break windshields, tear out seats
to feast on chips and greasy fries.

Near Warwoman Dell
the sound of a needling rain
turns to parchment every leaf
that falls.

EACH WE LOSE

for a friend who committed suicide

Each we lose takes a part
until we are left, not only bereft
but less, until at last we are lace
blowing in the wind, feathery ghosts
moving like tattered flowers,
jasmine with its cloying breath,
or sea foam that hisses on sand
and disappears.

When life is through with us,
there will be little for death to take,
a wisp of air. Close-mouthed,
one with a terrible sadness
you never shared,
you were not fair,
for you took more
than we ever planned.

My friend, my hovering spirit,
who left us without a word
nothing absolved, nothing solved,
no slash of pain can cover
your smile nor the breathless chatter
that left us enthralled. You are here yet,
that surge of life too real
for death to take it all.

STANDING HERE I SEE HILLS BEYOND HILLS

Ridge after ridge fades into gold,
and clouds drop low between each one
until there are white rivers
of fog measuring the valleys
and a haze of autumn trees
here and there or a deeper green
paling into strata that streak
the rain-washed light.
This is home: Appalachia
whispering its names: Cumberland,
Desolation Creek, Harlan
red with blood of miners,
Kay Jay, Artemus—
all form horizons that once led
pioneers and wanderers
to find singing voices, sirens' songs,
in these damp, winding ways.
Now as darkness falls and streams
thunder over flat rocks
with cooling rush and roar,
snakes curl down,
rattle and glide,
just as something stirs within,
some urge toward life
always out of reach, some other vista
just over there out of sight,
dim as the first faint stars.

KARMA, KISMET, FATE

destiny that preordains
the winding ways we take,
all lead to a grassy realm
rich beyond all plans,
wider than we could have known
on well-worn paths, these
mountain vistas pointing
to the stars, to the moon,
to endless skies and worlds
now beyond our ken
that tantalize and puzzle
and lead us on. Wherever
we go, I'll meet you there.

BELIEF

Late but here, spring returns
with less meaning now,
winter having taught
simplicity of stone and water,
bare branches sketched
in black and silver.
The lushness of birdsong days
cannot convince, for we have grown wise,
knowing fall's last breath
is frost, steely and unflinching.
Winter makes a splendor of fields
and yellow grass, holds
a light unknown by sodden moss.
Footsteps echo on unyielding ground.
How can we trust such a small sun?
How can we believe in warmth
or tomorrow or another year?

HOPE

Nothing lasts
and each is alone,
this is the smile
that grins in bone;
this is all I am told
and yet

beyond all evidence,
beyond the grave,
when all is taken,
when nothing endures,
the faintest star burns on.

In other galaxies
there are many suns,
other earths,
a parallel universe.
I see you alive,
in every one.

FIELD OF FLOWERS

In the middle of a field, a tree
and scattered about its feet,
rickrack of clover and buttons of flowers,
golden-eyed daisies, blue-green meadow-grass,
spread as if some careless seamstress
had dropped them,
embroidery tangled and spilled,
or perhaps it was some sleeper
whose dream sailed like a bubble and floated there
or some careless artist
whose brushes flicked
here a bit of pink, there a splash
of yellow. If l could keep them,
I would unravel summer fragrance
or at least the sun, thread it
into a quilt of light
to warm winter dreams;
I would let the dreamer go
to make daisy chains
or find a gallery large enough
to hold such scenes—
daisies under a tree
and flowers.

THE WITCH OF WINN-DIXIE

A quarter, a nickel, will that do?
The purse is cavernous,
and pennies get buried
somewhere in receipts
and scraps that have lost
their meaning. Crumbs vie
with bird seed, a broken stick of gum.

Behind her, the line stretches.
The cashier tries to smile and fails.
Are you going to take my cart out?
When you are ready, the boy says,
each word a stone.
He is bagging for someone else.

Once she taught botany,
how species vanish from the earth.
Her groceries in the cart at last,
she forgets him and leaves,
still sorting out dimes
and pennies, wondering
what tendrils and roots
tomorrow may bring,

some new pain perhaps
like a comet ready to explode—
store, clerk, coupons and specials,
bananas and apples
and her black purse,
blown to smithereens.

No one notices her cackling
across the parking lot,
trying to control
a wobbling wheel,
the squeak of rubber
on hot concrete.

TO STITCH A SUMMER SKY

Nothing to leave,
not talented with brush or needle,
I could not create those thick quilts
with starry patterns or lacy crochet
or cross-stitch to frame. Nothing
of dainty stitchery, splashes
of forests or watercolor
trees and lakes to mat and keep.
But look at the seams, see the traces
of blood, rust-colored, where I pricked a finger?
See how intricately the pattern is made?
I stitch a summer sky, grass
over graves, wild flowers scattered
like rain upon a moss-banked stream.
I leave for you these dreams,
to warm you on cold nights,
to wrap you when you feel alone or cold
and cannot sleep. Memories, wind in the eaves,
rattle of sleet upon the panes,
firelight shadows, scent of pine and cedar—
all I had and so for you, these.

THERE IS A LAND OF THE LIVING

homage to Thornton Wilder

I.
So briefly
that quick green
just at that second
when the sun disappears,
and then nothing
except the way
the surf sounds,
and the clouds glow,
sun-caught.

So this brief fire,
pulse and breath,
shall leave behind
no sound, no tinge
of sea or cloud,
little at all of beauty
or remembrance,
less than a sky
lingering with flame;

yet we are told,
though faith's faint edge
may slip away,
there is within us
a kind of splendor
we fail to see,
a green, gold purity
that will rise beyond the rim
of dying day.

II.
It returns, in the midst of snow and ice,
in the midst of destruction, decay,
when hope spreads its wings
and covers its young; when the last shell
fails to open, it is there, finding no despair
that will not lessen, no spring
that fails or autumn or star that flames
across the sky that does not appear
and will. The tiny twig, less than a whip,
has at its heart that pale tint and the sea breathes
its deep sigh, slinging itself against the rocks
of all the lies that never last,
gray-green algae that fades away.

We wait as upon a rampart
and see the dying sun, knowing it
again will rise, and as one drowning
who will not let go, we cling
to every thread of light that spreads
across the moon. Frail as a web
that wavers over death's deepest chasm,
that swinging bridge, love.

SUNDAY CHICKEN, '42

Though the Depression had faded,
thrift was ingrained.
Three blocks from the square,
Mrs. Partin milked her cow.
Nothing would be the same.
Nothing was wasted.
Cornfields wrapped the house
like a blanket.

We wiped sweat, used electric fans.
A square of cotton tied
to the screen door
kept blue-bottles from the house
as they swarmed from chicken yard
and hog pens. Grandma's fly-spray
pumped the porch to life again
at sundown.

Mountain fogs rolled in
to the rasp of jarflies, tree frogs,
TB and asthma. Typhoid's miasma
probed creek banks and cesspools.
Morning glories wrapped corn stalks,
while polio was rampant as vines.

Saturdays Grandma whirled
a white leghorn by the neck,
sent it flopping,
And I, faintly sick, spellbound,
sat in a chair by the dishpan
as she removed
gizzard, liver, iridescent guts—
all forgotten at Sunday's table,
awash in gravy and greasy fingers.

At night I turned the pillow
to sleep cool, listening to stalks
rustle like pages in an album,
the slow whisper of tassels
in a warm rag of wind.
Death haunted restless dreams
in clouds of blood and feathers.

THE BLACKENED HEARTH

No fire burns here, not even the comfortable glow
of one banked to hold till a morning when cold
breaks at the windows. Yet they are so close;
they are comrades, grown battle-weary with time,
too little laughter, the slow wearing away
of too many troubles too young.
The smothering ash of circumstance,
pain, loss—all these have rounded their shoulders,
dulled their eyes, made them despair.

Neither can blame the other, though they recall
the teasing ember of touch,
the gaze that reached deep
to where they were, that drew them out
like a fire drawn by an updraft, roaring
and alive. Now they gaze across the room,
past each other, across the bond of habit,
the history that has brought them here,
to these frozen years, where they stare
into a blackened hearth.

DEPTHS

Dark plum tints the evening sky
and overhead a pale moon floats,
a blossom on water.

So too your eyes,
blue shadows of deep water
and on the surface my face.

A TWIG HAS TOLD ME

The wind moaned over the fields;
I thought I heard some sound
whose source I could not discern,
some grackle frozen, unable to move
or a small lost mouse. It was no night
to be about, not where phantoms walk
or ice gives way to drown
hapless creatures in the darkness of the pond.

It was no night for man to wander far
from hearth and home or become aware
of a universe so star-blasted, so remote
that gases wrap great galaxies,
and nothing touches at all,
not planets nor stars, only black holes
where neutrons collide, nitrogen explodes.
This is no world for life at all.

And so I came home and thought,
until above my mantel,
caught in the light of the fire, I saw
heather budding in a brown vase,
a plain vase colorless as my soul,
out of season, out of place,
swellings on a twig, and here and there
a small green leaf, and like a fool

I found myself cheering,
saying, "Go on, go on."
The wind howled around the corners,
but I did not care, neither was I afraid.
Bud, grackle and mouse—
all struggle in the balance, myself as well;
all are helpless in an infinity so cold,
so vast, I wonder if God can hear me,
if there is any god to care,
yet a twig has told me
something small and green shall last,
and something in that telling
warms the winter doubt.

OCTOBER CORTEGE: New Orleans

Streamers, gold and green and crimson,
flash in the sun as bugles
of brass and bronze send throngs
high-stepping through the streets
on their return with the saints.

Forgotten now
those long, low mournful songs,
black crepe and tears
that wound their way
behind a swaying hearse.

Marchers feign happiness
with such color, celebration, yet
nothing masks winter waiting
on the corner nor the drums that echo
under all.

We shiver in a fickle wind,
the drift of leaves, old papers and dust,
laugh and cry oh laugh and cry
with jazz and jubilation,
in October's last cortege

honoring a painted lady
carried home.

VIGNETTE

Bare trees, white hills, and snow,
a flake or two blown from a drift
beside the road, a moon riding high,
cold. Winter floats a foggy breath
in curls of smoke that cling to roofs,
hang low, then join a cloud
with sparks borne upon an updraft.
Windows glow. Inside, the family sits,
in quiet companionship. There is no sound
except the shift of logs, a ticking clock.
The house is beating like a heart.
Christmas descends with white wings,
the scent of apples and evergreens,
and above the house in darkest night,
the milky foam of stars.

STAR GAZER

Memories ago, I wished on stars,
the first one of the evening
rising over Sampson Hill,
counted them and pondered other worlds.
That summer I was fourteen,
and death had little meaning,
no more than stars, distant and dying.
To me they were wishes,
vague yearnings flickering
like fireflies on the lawn.
In August heat, unable to sleep,
I watched the Perseid,
poor wishes streaking across the sky.
When you are fourteen, no one dies.

Tonight they have come again,
making no sound, yet I think
of how they should sound,
a faint pock, pock,
like stones thrown in pools,
small bubbles of sound,
or howitzers upon some fire-bombed hill.
But they are silent.
They are souls arriving and departing,
carrying their wishes with them
in brief, bright flames,
and they have gone like the deep, clear eyes
of one who watched them flare and fall.

HUMMINGBIRD

An iridescence
in the dawn
flits from flower to flower,
takes a sip of nectar
from a rose, tumbles a daisy,
jostles the bee,
hums a hymn
to summer and to brevity.
He hovers in a zigzag,
darts and disappears.
We gasp and breathe
and wonder… did we see him at all
or did a rainbow shatter
or a jewel explode?

HOME

On the porch a dog rolls on his back, paws up.
Wind chimes ring with a watery sound,
and a jay clangs from the popcorn tree.
Two fat bees lurch from tea olive
to jasmine then back again.
Music wafts from the windows;
a voice calls within, and someone replies.
This is a humble world,
this little house on this little street.
There isn't much here
that anyone would want, except peace.
When all is gone,
will anyone know the spot? Likely not.
But the bees may come again
and of course the wind.
Perhaps like a breeze far at sea
that carries a trace of inland flowers
the air will carry across the years
a faint sense of what was ours.
Evening again will descend, settling in
like small birds coming home.

STUFF

Spores of yeast
grow into a fur or frieze.
Dry rot,
though, leaves
no sign until
stuff is touched;
then lace or cloth,
having too much sun,
too much furnace,
falls into powder.
The soil of living
is ground in.
Bones, too, and hair and nails,
all the kingdoms of this world,
the young, the fair, fall
into detritus or decay.
Yet we gather and love
lace, wood, the leavings of tombs,
and leave of ourselves
a grain or two to blow
upon the wind, a few words,
just whispering breaths, to say
"We are such…
As dreams are made…"

ONCE MORE IN PASSING

for my daughter

Today in the mall,
thirty years vanished
as I saw you in passing,
and I stopped and stared.
Everything came back again,
all those others of you I lost too,
The Christmases, the gladness,
your first steps, those soulful
solemn eyes I could never see
to the bottom of,
your little perspiring nose
when you were afraid of doctors' offices
and shots, and that red hat tied under your chin
when I took you to swing in the park,
then those troubled years
when you threatened to run away,
played rock till I could scream,
and loved your father but not me.
Only seen from the back,
only seen in passing,
jeans now retro seventies,
frayed and dragging at the hem,
and your dark hair
straight, shining—
how many there have been,
those strangers seen across a room
or swimming in a pool,
bringing their time-warp yesterdays,
unaware, happy,
in a crowd, or as just now
going into a store, laughing.
And no one hears me as I say,
"Oh, Leslie…"

VII

Almost Home

WHAT KIND OF MIRACLE

brushed upon his breast
the palest tangerine
and covered his small head
with such a sunset glow
of palest orange;
what kind of miracle
penciled his gray wings
with a thin line

then placed him here,
pine grosbeak, silly
and ordinary name,
precariously perched
on a twig of crab apple,
frozen fruit and gray limbs
a perfect match for him
who feasts upon the watery
salvage of fall;

what kind
of miracle made them alike,
twig limbs wrapped around twigs,
amber eyes alert and deep
with amber darkness of cold?
I do not know. I only see
a jewel placed upon a jewel,
pine grosbeak in a crab apple tree.

FLAKES OF MOONLIGHT

I.
Hold upon your tongue the faint clear bell
of a bird mourning its mate
and know whatever comes shall go,
shall become flat and dull; but now,
recall in spring, the sheen of sun
on grass and how a sun-burned boy
kissed you when you found
wild strawberries hidden under leaves,
and gave you wild, wild kisses more and more.
Remember how a hook of moon
in April caught a star

and scythed brown fields in autumn,
hay bound and left, green-tinged.
All circled, came again.
Now in firelight's waning,
breathe the faint musk of his skin.
Know, as only one alone can know,
wordless peace in dying flames,
seasons rich as summer wine,
full and warm with rain, though snow
is falling like a thousand moons
catching in black branches of the apple tree.

II.
Though the moon rides high and cold
in a cloudless sky,
it is snowing everywhere.
Dogwood blossoms float
and peach and pear,
and woodbine drops yellow gold
without a sound. Early roses, too,
petal down, waft fragrance
in ghostly flakes upon the air.

Goblin flowers spring up in shadows
where none appeared before
where violets cling to earth
wrapped in heart-shaped shawls.
Something is happening in stillness
and in stealth. A breath blows
one bloom from the tulip tree,
uncurls one leaf—there and there.
On a balcony someone still calls,
and far away a small voice is lost
in centuries of springs and frost

III.
Winter put away like woolens,
summer lovers lie in dunes and gaze,
feel the tug and pull,
nebulous as that cold face,
pearlescent, pale with the anemia
of its own stare, its bland indifference.

They are silent, dazzled
by the crackle of light on water,
lost in the sound of roaring thunder and
    withdrawal,
not unlike the release of love, that surrender.
Every spreading breaker hisses into foam.

Above a darkness too deep to measure,
flakes of moonlight rise and fall.

LORD OF ALL SEASONS

His laugh dimples the birdbath.
His footsteps scatter the seeds.
Cockleburs cling to his gown;
and in the star burst of weeds,
we see his crown. In autumn mist
the benediction of his breath
brings the fallen leaf to rest.

Snow flocks the stones
where worn lambs guard
sleeping children far below.
In that piercing cold he alone
knows the beating heart of time
is warm beyond this place
and small are the steps of grace.

Crumbs of earth, leaf mold, move
like hands groping from a grave;
sun and rain speak resurrection
in a language soft and plain,
a Quaker thee, a nun's vow,
promises kept in all that's green
and a meadow filled with flowers.

Beetles return, the ugly worm,
a tent of endless days,
and all the armies of the sun
attest that swollen beans and fruits and nests
go on. The blackbird and his brothers
take a sip of rain-wet lawn. From a poplar,
wind chimes greet the dawn.

CIRCUMFERENCE

I knew by heart every tree root
that buckled the sidewalks,
the view from the river bridge,
the Cumberland in its slow
muddy ribbon,
Sharp's Gap, the cemetery,
the brickyard ponds,
College Street,
North Main, Allison Avenue,
Manchester Street. A labyrinth
unwound in a flurry
of winged maple seeds, lady bugs
who left their children at home.

I knew dogs, called them
by name or went the other way.
Words formed in a wonderment
of clear lungs, strong legs.
Cracks in the pavement, potholes,
gravel were my consonants.
Hedges, broken fences
and a dazzle of blossoms
twisted like a vine
of melodious vowels
through my veins.
Sweet speech of all those days
I walked and remember.

AUBADE FOR THE FIRST COOL DAY

Rain-beguiled, daft with delight,
sharing perhaps adagios
wafting through the door,
who knows what impels
a mockingbird to greet
September in trill
after trill, as he balances
on a limb where caterpillars
sway in their nested chambers
waiting to play havoc
with my lawn?

Alive oh alive, so full of yourself,
crazy bird, senseless and wise,
your lyrics scatter gold
upon my pauper page.

I cannot know
the source of such joy,
such fullness of heart
or stomach or small bird lungs.
I only know rippling arpeggios,
and the first of fall
in shadows that crisscross
the book I close, and where I,
caught and amazed, hear a rapture
beyond my capacity to share.

FORGOTTEN SONG

One by one by one, they are going:
the young, the beautiful, the brave.
And yesterday the same, over centuries—
the earth is seeded with my kin,
and suddenly from nowhere it seems
there rises a need, inchoate and painful
as the memory of something that can't be
    named,
a lost, forgotten song:

the mountains and those who came,
who traveled by ship to reach rich valleys
where they lie, under stone,
crumbling markers, unsung,
yet I hear their singing bones,
and that ache within calls names:
Roanoke, Coeburn, Dungannon,
Clinch Mountain, Bean Station.

Jacob and Jalah Wolfe, their children,
all who worked the land
and salted it with their sweat,
I sing you now in dirge and dulcimer.
Can you hear me humming in the trees
or see me in the leaves deep
upon those weed-choked graves?
Home, cousins, kin, listen:
I am there.

WITNESS

Think of the lily and the dandelion,
the curve of a swan's neck
and the mountain-goat's horns.
Examine all things
sublime and mundane,
both the puddle and the lake
pocked with rain.

Look at how all things are made,
the tiger and the tabby,
the worm and the asp,
whatever is thick or sparse,
complex or plain,
the red dwarf, the gnat,
my hands, your eyes,
the fist of a baby
filling its mouth.

Find true north and a pinpoint star.
Finally think of faces,
soldiers' young faces
as unique as fingerprints.
One-by-one someone's world is gone.
Then ask, "Father-God,
what does all this mean?"

Silence,
and a flake of snow across a pane.

I AM CLEANING OUT MY LIFE

remembering Anne George

Anne, there are no pieces
of dried ham to cut my finger,
but there are books I barely remember
with poetry as bad as that ham,
poets' names I cannot recall;
one-by-one I am tossing them.
If I cannot stand the guilt,
there are charities; let them
make the awful choices.
Here is one by a poet I do not like.
It is not his poetry, just him.

Here is one filled with death wishes,
finally a suicide. It has to go.
Oh, it feels good, doing this.
Take that, and that!
Akin to an emotional rape?
In a way. There are no bags
of green liquid, but the poets
have *multiplied*.
Do they reproduce?
Who is he? Who is she?

God knows many were remaindered.
How came they to be
in this refrigerator of poetry?
I am reveling in their demise. GO! GO!
And if someone should toss me?
I deserve it for the cackling fire
of my glee. Take your mixed metaphors.
Take your worn ideas, your obscurity.
I am cleaning out my life.

PRIMAL

Faintly at night, sometimes
there is scratching at the door.
Whatever it is wants in.
Beyond the pool of light,
alone in the snow,
something is watching, eyes yellow
as the lantern by the barn.
It wants what we have,
to be where we are,
shut in our cozy house,
our bright circle of talk.
Tail lashing, it paces, lurks,
squats just on the edge of dark.
Attentive, we pause, listen,
then hurry on, eager to ignore
the breath of cold
that seems to slide under the door,
aware we cannot make it disappear
with all our brave chatter, with all our fire
or light or talk of tomorrow.
Beyond reasoning, beyond prayer,
it is out there
unsheathing its claws.

THE FOURTH WITCH

So come, Greymalkin,
I know you well
as other fiends I know in hell,
know the windings of your heart
the alleys where you dwell.
My familiar, the caldron's darkest depths
are not so dark as this world's ways.
Do your work. I'll cast my spell,
go with you from tomb to tomb
stealing bones of babe and brute,
sipping mother's blood, ichor
sweet of suicides.

Come, Greymalkin, spirit, sprite,
bring in lightning, bring in night.
Move now from my cottage door,
claws unsheathed and eyes aglow,
wrapped in blackness, cloaked in filth.
Come inside and greet your friend.
Then let us roam, two alike,
over moor and woodland gloom.
Both as foul as entrails' stench,
I shall chant and you shall cry,
wake the sleepers as they toss,
wench and lout, greased in lust.

NIGHTHAWKS

In darkness lit only by the glare
from seamless windows,
we are staring into a corner café
where two coffee urns reflect
fluorescence
as cold as these faces—
one counter man, three customers—
each looking slantwise or down.
No one touches.
No one talks.
It could be any time,
any street, any place,
a planet circling some dying star.
It may be two A.M.; it may be New York
or Chicago.
We've all been there:
in that space
where people wait
for something, someone,
blind yet alert,
nighthawks that circle
in a pocket of light.

REGRET

Ten million words
whistle in the wind,
words unsaid or spoken.
Rage that should never have been,
black and sere as curled leaves.
There is no going back to say
what we should have said,
to touch your face
and speak with my eyes
or feel your skin,
to calm your shaking hands,
to name you
friend or mother
or lover or sweetheart.
And so only floating regrets,
this ache that chokes
in a constricted throat
and pinches a selfish heart.
Dead vines wind
around winter trees.
Listen to the wind.
Useless as yesterday,
it babbles and goes on.

REMEMBER

Pinpoints of nuclear fire, a friend said,
and assigned no special
significance except change
and time. Not even God.
Not even wonder.

But coming home late I was caught by surprise
as when a child who tried to visualize their size,
constellations still in place,
though now I knew a name or two.

I looked toward Orion
and searched for the North Star
and that place, true north,
starless and black as…
not death…
rather the lack of anyone to remember
the small burning center
of a child grown old,
one who loves anew
the cold black night,
each wavering planet,
even that empty space.
where no stars are.

MAYBE THE WAY DEATH IS

Finally to know again
a small house on a small street,
the sound of voices saying my name;
to hear in the night a train

winding toward a future
that has come to be
speeding toward an end
I shall not know until I arrive,

breathless and alone,
like a child afraid of ghosts
from telling stories past dark,
then running over summer lawns

toward the yellow lights of home.

LILACS

The scent of lilacs in spring,
the way
they tremble in a light rain,
the way
they shake down
upon my wrist their sweetness.
Never another
day like this
nor shall I ever be
as young again, so alive,

watching the watery sun appear
to touch with fire
each separate leaf,
each separate blossom,
nor shall I love
again in just this way, my breath
rising like a faint perfume
fanning out
upon the air, to caress with muted words—
your heart, your hands, your hair.

So many springs,
but never the same, like the girl
who never said or heard you say
words frail as lilacs
frothy and bowed with rain.

ANNIVERSARY

The hotel long gone, destroyed,
but then, we had a corner room
that caught the sun.
You, nineteen, I, just seventeen,
and upon the dresser your Air Force hat,
mine beside it, "Lucy" style, straw-molded
    into a pancake
with wings and white veil. Underneath,
your black shoes, my new white ones, linen.

That morning,
both of us wondering, half-asleep,
and realizing we were not alone,
nor would we ever be again.
Once we talked about growing old
and laughed. Not us, somehow not us.
My plain gold ring held more gold
than we owned.

The Sunday paper read and scattered,
we went to the bus station for breakfast.
No car, nothing at all to spare
except time that stretched like wrinkled sheets,
crumpled papers, and the voice of Johnny Ray
singing "Cry" over the jukebox.
A voice called out departures.

ALMOST HOME

Looking down, you will think we are there,
under six feet of Alabama clay.
Don't ever think it. That is dust.

All of us—Sam, Leslie, me—
we left here long ago,
and you will not find us

except in fog above Autauga Creek
or closer to childhood's home,
marveling at bluegrass

or picking blackberries
just to see their shine
or you'll see our traces deep

in muddy Cumberland banks
where we fished
when we were young.

More than likely though
you will see little but wind
lifting a leaf, or hear some bird

far away singing in an updraft,
tilting one wing and free.
That little breath will be us,

lingering as long as we can,
held to earth by mountains,
streams, bound here for love
of all we knew and you.

VIII

New Poems

THIS ONE DAY

This rich, wet, autumn day, with all it apple-seeded
cider gold
if it were mine, and you were mine, and we two
could hold this glistening fruit we once knew
then life would never end. If I held again
your hand and walked those winding roads
those hills, those trees laden, limbs touching the ground
with harvest
and hay-rolled and left in fields, so barley-green
and if we knew...
what time would bring...what would we do?
We would bless the streams that make their way
through mountain valleys, and walk through mist
and nothing could find us or hurt us and not even
the wind of winter
could make us change, grow old, go away.
Only time would die. But never this autumn day.

DICHOTOMIES

Rain-washed, in full bloom
roses, beaded, perfumed, cast their souls
upon the first soft winds of spring.
Life is like this,
but it is also mud swirling in the gutters,
children brandishing guns,
the elderly left alone,
cells dying in their brains.
The dichotomy of living is all of these:
worms and wings, love wilting under the sway
of lust, all things good and evil,
earth that flows with fire and wrath and martyrs' blood.
Struck dumb by complexity and pain,
we must find our way to faith,
peddlers lost in the marketplace,
hawking winter's worn and shabby wares, side by side
with spring's first flowers
bent with praise and rain.

WHEN THE INK RAN DRY

and the paper ran out
and all the doors had been closed
and words wouldn't come
I stepped outside to stare
at the speechless stars,
aloof, pristine, and unaware of pain.
There is not enough ink to hold grief,
and no poem can contain the whole of joy
or even a sprig of what it means to be alive,
and here on the edge of an abyss,
defeated, yet triumphant,
I laughed and breathed the deep dark
mystery of the Milky Way,
wanting only to write the sky.

Index of Poems

INDEX OF POEMS

A Bouquet for Leslie	194	A Whirling in the Stars	203
Absence	111	A Winter Tea	316
Absolution	62	Balm	240
Adagio for Voice and Strings	218	Beach Fires	239
After a Long Absence	132	Bearing the Print	282
A Gift of Potatoes	134	Before These Mountains	48
A House Beyond Repair	136	Beginning	50
Alabama Autumn	9	Belief	327
Alchemy	142	Beyond Survival	314
All Those Mornings	269	Biology, Night School	27
Almost Home	366	Blackstar	65
Always Eve	8	Broken Trust	207
Ancient Fire: Kentucky's First House	232	Buffalo Bill at the Piggly Wiggly	169
An Empty Vase	197	Bus	44
A Night of Bingo, Mountain City, Georgia	168	Camellias	166
Anniversary	365	Canticle in September	235
Another Picture	115	Carapace	146
Another Room	254	Ceremony of Names	98
April 12, 1945	228	Chalice	19
April Reunion	137	Cherokee Autumn	242
A Scent of Green	141	Christina's World	241
A Sea Journey	108	Circle of Light	183
A Simple Thing	52	Circumference	353
Aspects	6	City Cemetery	56
At an Auction, Maybe	202	Cold Comfort	180
A Turn of Seasons	266	Conjunctions	167
A Twig Has Told Me	338	Cool Water	274
Aubade for the First Cool Day	354	Copper Harbor	303
August Morning	284	Dangers Past	143
Aurora Borealis	54	Dark Honey	14
Autumn Aubade	49	Days of the Crone	93
Autumn, Don't	4	Death of a Critic	46
Autumn Snow	257	Death of a Tree	38
		Depths	337

Descendant	278
Désolé	13
Dichotomies	370
Disappearances	306
Each We Lose	325
Each Year and Always	311
Early Autumn, 1944	69
Elemental	88
Encounter	42
End of August	52
End of the Workshop	43
Facing the Audience	176
Fallow	148
Feast	296
Feather in the Wind	185
February, '63	170
Field of Flowers	329
First Father's Day	113
First Reader, Politically Incorrect	165
First Song	304
Fishing for God	204
Flakes of Moonlight	350
Flash of Green	299
Fool's Gold	159
Forgiveness	293
Forgotten Song	355
For Lack of Words	25
For William Matthews	298
Fresh Laundry	130
Frost Study	250
Funerals	72
Furnished Tombs	112
Genesis	173
Ghost Story	116
Gone	16
Good Water	174
Grace	117
Grace Notes	302
Grass	216
Hambidge Woods	213
Hansel and Gretel at the Beach	90
Harvest	91
Haunted	104
Hawk Above the Highway	86
Held in Amber	121
Hester and Arthur	84
Home	344
Hope	328
Household Accounts	101
Hummingbird	343
I Am Cleaning Out My Life	357
If I Were a Poet	310
Ignis Fatuus	18
Indian Summer	144
In North Georgia Near Warwoman Dell	324
Instructions	164
Intermission	227
In the Twentieth Century	84
It Isn't Poverty	85
It Must Have Been in Autumn	94
Karma, Kismet, Fate	327
Last Winter	256
Late Spring: The Widow Speaks	261
Leaven	78
Less than Greek	102
Libation	147
Lilacs	364
Literary Tea	28
Live Coals	66
Lord of All Seasons	352

Lost Trove: Appalachia 131	On Such a Day 192
Love and a Season 155	Orion 226
Love Out of Time,	Our Lives are Tangled 26
Out of Season 294	Overnight the World
Magnolias 149	Had Changed 320
Massacre 29	Oxfordshire 97
Maybe the Way Death Is 363	Pagoda Village 182
Meditation at Summer's End . 243	Patchwork 222
Merlin on Poetry 313	Pay Telephone 12
Montage 35	Perception 224
Montgomery 79	Perils of a Southern Gothic
Moss on the North Side 265	Childhood 122
Mother to Child 24	Perspective, Powell Valley . . . 118
Mountain Battle 153	Poetry Teacher 175
Mountain Child 20	Point, Counterpoint 15
Mountain Fog 133	Portent 281
My Thin Gold Grandmother . . 22	Preserves 59
Nativity on Roosevelt Street . 126	Primal 358
Newspaper Photo, 1920 107	Processional in Gray 262
Night College 171	Prodigals 92
Night Cry 114	Regret 361
Night Fishing 103	Remember 362
Nighthawks 360	Remembering Zelda 81
Night on Craig Mountain . . . 127	Remembrance 187
Night Watch 186	Returning 68
No Sanctuary 61	Revelation 292
No Stolen Fire 220	Revisions 238
November Rain 109	Ripples 41
October Cortege:	Roadside Crosses 70
New Orleans 340	Ruffed Grouse Beneath 249
Old Sins 286	Shepherds at Midnight
On a Kentucky Hill 206	Remember 246
On Buying a Sprig of Quince . 150	Show and Tell 39
Once More in Passing 346	Signature: The Deep South . . 295
Once More This Fire 319	Silences 263
Only the Locusts 151	Simple Things 74
On Meeting a Chameleon . . . 163	Singing Where We Are 188

Skate Song 124	The Gentle Way of Earth 110
Snake 152	The History of a Yellow Leaf . 312
Soliloquy of the Rose 287	The Key 17
Something's Out There 77	The Last Drive-In
Soundless 309	In America Closes 129
Speak to Me 5	The Lesson 32
Spindrift 36	The Lost Children 208
Splitting the Melon 33	The Lovers 179
Spring Rain 154	The Memory Box 40
Spring, Rain, Laughter 53	The Picture Window 249
Standing Here I See 326	The Pleiades 55
Star Children 96	The Radio 80
Star Gazer 342	There Is a Land of the Living . . 332
Storm 47	The River 51
Storm's End 264	These Weeds 3
Strawberrie Banckes 100	The Sorcerers 128
Stuff 345	The Source 140
Sunday Chicken, '42 334	The Storyteller 190
Susurrus 87	The Tallow Tree 37
Tao 158	The Traveler 277
Test 285	The Typing Pool v10
Testament 234	The Waiting Room 58
That October Night 308	The Way I Write 12
The Art of Winning 300	The Witch Of Winn-Dixie . . 330
The Baptist Ladies Meet at	This Easter, Nashville 230
Quincy's 161	This One Day 369
The Baptist Ladies Travel to	Ticket, $2.50 46
the Factory Outlets 82	Tidal 255
The Blackened Hearth 336	Tidal Marsh 244
The Bond (For Leslie) 31	Time Capsule 105
The Cedar 245	Toadstools 34
The Cheerleader 162	To a Fertilizer Salesman From
The Children of Summer . . . 253	Laurel, Mississippi 160
The Created 248	To Love 219
The Feather 252	Tongues of Flame 178
The Food Bearers 106	To Stitch a Summer Sky 331
The Fourth Witch 359	To the Fittest in the Office 30

Travelers	172
Triptych for Autumn	270
Used Clothes	276
Vanishing	201
Vignette	341
Voice Among the Trees	199
Voices	280
Watercolor	76
Watermelon Moon	138
What Dreams May Come	315
What Kind of Miracle	349
What Stays With Us	323
What the Moon Knows	258
What the Roses Say	198
What the Wind Knew	196
What You Were	200
When Birds Return	305
When Spring Touched with Fire	189
When the Ink Ran Dry	371
Whispers	214
White Marble	318
Widows' Walk	184
Wild Geese in Moonlight	251
Wind Chimes	60
Winter Apples	272
Winterscape	156
Winter's Tale	290
Without Shelter	288
Witness	356
Yard Sale	83
Yellow Creek	73

A Little About Sue Scalf

Sue spent her childhood travelling with her parents and attending schools in Kentucky, Tennessee, Virginia, and Ohio—fifteen different schools—before marrying in the summer after the eleventh grade. She graduated from high school in Hampton, Virginia and attended college at Michigan Tech and Troy State University in Alabama, where she graduated *summa cum laude* and earned a master's degree in English.

Travels with her Air Force husband included five years in Michigan, where he served with the Air Force ROTC program, a year near San Francisco, and three years in England. Sue lives now in Alabama. Until her retirement she taught middle school, high school, and college level courses in English, poetry, and creative writing.

Two of Sue's eight books of poetry were nominated for the Pulitzer Prize; four were named "Book of the Year" by the Alabama State Poetry Society. Hundreds of her poems have won awards (eight Hackney awards as well as the William Stafford Award) and have been published in literary journals such as *The Southern Review, The Southern Poetry Review, Cumberland Poetry Review, CrossConnect, Tar River Review, The English Journal,* and in a number of anthologies: *A Baker's Dozen: Contemporary Women Poets of Alabama; Alabama Poets: A Contemporary Anthology; Anthology One* (The Alsop Review Press); and *Southern Voices in Every Direction.* Her reviews and articles have appeared in *First Draft* and *Elk River Review.* In 2011, she won first prize and publication for her chapbook, *To Stitch a Summer Sky.*

www.ingramcontent.com/pod-product-compliance
Lightning Source LLC
Chambersburg PA
CBHW061953180426
43198CB00036B/784